Other writings by Dalan E. Smith:
> *Bill & I: Building William Shatner's Belle Reve Ranch*

Copyright 2013, Dalan E. Smith
All rights reserved

ISBN-13: 978-1490319490
ISBN-10: 1490319492

Printed by CreateSpace, an Amazon.com Company

THINGS I'VE LEARNED FROM MY BIRD DOGS
(and other good friends)

By Dalan E. Smith

*To Bob —
A long-time and to be longer-time friend —
Dalan Smith*

DEDICATION

To Jared Evans, whose enthusiasm as a child for the earliest of my bird dog stories stoked the embers of a fire that glowed until this project came to fruition.

THINGS I'VE LEARNED FROM MY BIRD DOGS
(and other good friends)

by Dalan E. Smith

TABLE OF CONTENTS

Foreword   9

THE "OLD CHRIS" ERA
1. Dog Paddle   14
2. Old Chris' Real Name   16
3. Tolerance   18
4. Better Than Christmas   20
5. First Wild Fish   22
6. Don't Jump   23
7. The Loyalty of Old Chris   25
8. Uncle Hebe   27
9. Run!   30
10. Chris' Wild Goose Chase   32
11. Salmon River, East Fork Camp   35
12. Old Sinner   37
13. Dad's Snake   39
14. Enthusiasm, Used and Misused   42
15. Favorite Holiday   44

THE "BUTCH" ERA
16. Patience Has Its Rewards   47
17. Butch's High-Speed Adventure   49
18. Gradual Growth   50
19. Night Wanderer   52
20. Smells Like Gas in Here!   54
21. The Last Old-Fashioned Haystack   56
22. Clarabelle and a Shady Tree   59
23. Meadow Creek   62

24. A Real Good Hunting Horse	65
25. Avoid the Very Appearance of Danger, Or Operating on the Edge	67
26. Black Canyon	69
27. Black Canyon in Winter	72
28. Keith in Black Canyon	74
29. Largest Trout	75
30. First Goose	77

INTERIM PERIOD I

31. Seagull 4th of July	80
32. Uncle Lew's Goose Hunt	82
33. Fat Dogs and Good Wives	84
34. Fairview Deer	85
35. The Pfeifferhorn	87
36. The Non-Bird Dog	90
37. Ask, Listen	92
38. Opportunity	94
39. Sam	96

THE "RUFUS" ERA

40. Bird Dog in Training	99
41. Rufus, a Good Dad	102
42. Brother-in-Law's Goose	104
43. Bigfoot Lives at Bloomington Lake	105
44. Tulip Crossed Up	108
45. Persistence Delivers	111
46. Look Before You Leap	113
47. Sandhill Crane Goose	116
48. Joe the Horse	117
49. Rufus' Baby Duck	120
50. The Beginning of an Era	122
51. A Horse Buy Mistake	125
52. Rufus and the Coyote Trap	128
53. "Humanizing" a Foal	130

54. Blue Eyes	132
55. Why Bird Dogs Smell	134
56. Publicity Shots	136
57. Revising a TJ Hooker Script	138
58. A Missing Baby	140
59. A Friendly Wave	142
60. Talented Rufus	143

INTERIM PERIOD II

61. Not-So-Wily Coyote	146
62. Demonstration of Muscle	147
63. First Hollow	149
64. The Grass is Always Greener?	152
65. The Abundance Mentality	154
66. Drivers	156
67. Fishing Practice	157

THE "CHIP" ERA

68. Choosing a Bird Dog	161
69. Watermelon Chip	163
70. Grouse for Dinner	164
71. Internal Clock	166
72. Gift Fish for Breakfast	168
73. Jackson Hole	170
74. Cultural Differences	172
75. Horses and Fences	173
76. Friendship	176
77. A Parable by a Dog	179
78. A Medical Lesson	181
79. Adrenaline Rush	183
80. Gyrations of Gratitude	185
81. Grandma Smith	187

The incidents in chapters 50, 51, 52, 53, 54, 56, 57, 58, and 60 were formerly published in similar form in *Bill and I: Building William Shatner's Belle Reve Ranch,* by Dalan E. Smith

THINGS I'VE LEARNED FROM MY BIRD DOGS
(and other good friends)
by Dalan E. Smith

Foreword

Most of my life I have been blessed with the friendship of good dogs. These were always bird dogs, the retriever breeds, and also a mix of breeds, as they seem to be best at being friends, great family dogs, a lot less hyper than purebreds, and more laid back and easier to train, thus bringing the most pleasure. Life on a small farm in southern Idaho was made more pleasant by the sport of hunting, and game brought home to supplement groceries was welcome, and this was always most successful with the aid of a good dog. The rules of hunting were quite simple: always hunt in season, have proper licenses, waste nothing, shoot carefully to protect the meat, field dress and care for game properly, stay within bag limits, respect the property of others, leave gates as you find them, clean guns and equipment regularly, don't stay out so late that mother worries, and most importantly take good care of the bird dog.

I've heard it said that the personality of a dog is a reflection of the personality of the owner, especially when the owner is also the trainer, as was the case at our house. Over the years I've watched to verify this idea, and I concur. It doesn't seem to matter who learns from whom, but both are fed from the same development stream. One of the generally accepted myths is that dogs (and other animals) can't think or reason, but I disagree, as I've seen them stand and deliberately decide what was the best next move. Naturally, this brings me to realize that the ideas coming from my good friend and hunting companion may teach me something, and I have welcomed that tutoring.

Because of the nature of life, there have been times when I have been without a good bird dog, and I always felt there was something missing in those periods. The most influential and memorable of those dogs that have benefited my life are four special friends:

Chris, Springer Spaniel/Water Spaniel cross, the first dog I remember as a child;

Butch, German Shorthair/Water Spaniel cross, when I was a teenager;

Rufus, German Shorthair/Redbone Hound cross, (with son Chris) when Judy and I were first married;

and Chip, German Shorthair/Chocolate Lab cross, after our kids were grown.

With that said, this is a collection of events that have helped me develop a philosophy of life, and I am including lessons learned from my bird dogs and also from other animals and various experiences that have affected the development of my thought processes. One of the most important things I have realized is that, given a chance, there is something to be learned from every person, every creature, and every situation I experience in life.

THE "OLD CHRIS" ERA

Chapter 1
Dog Paddle

I must have been 3 or 4 when the family, including my three older sisters and both of my parents went to the swimming hole in the Bear River above the nearby bridge, not far below the mouth of the Oneida Narrows. When the river was low (the flow was regulated by the dam upstream at Oneida Station) we played in the swimming hole below the island and enjoyed the relative safety of the slow moving water. This particular day it was not low, but quite high and filled with strong currents. Old Chris, being part Water Spaniel, jumped in as usual, and enjoyed cooling off as he was swept downstream a few hundred feet to a shallow place and waded ashore. My older sisters got permission to jump in near the grassy bank just below the swimming hole and, under the watchful eye of Dad and Mother, paddled downstream with the current a little ways then crawled out on the bank.

Bear River just above the bridge

I apparently thought that swimming must be pretty good, so I decided I could do it too, but since I had not yet learned to swim I knew the folks would not let me try it. Somehow I had not recognized that swimming was necessary to staying on top of the water, even if the only stroke known was to dog paddle like Chris, so I unobtrusively walked upstream past everyone and then jumped in the river, careful to not let anyone see me do the forbidden act. The bank dropped off steep, the water was deep, and I immediately went under water and was swept downstream in the swift current. I don't know who saw me bob to the surface, but I do remember Dad pulling me from the water. I don't even think I was chastised, but nobody in our family who did something that dumb got off without some discipline. Looking back, I appreciate that I was spotted and retrieved, and it was a great lesson to me that I was not nearly as capable as the family bird dog and could perhaps learn something from him. This may have been the beginning of a lifetime of lessons, some of great importance and all significant, from my bird dogs and those around me.

Chapter 2
Old Chris' Real Name

Old Chris, as we called him, was the favorite friend of all us kids growing up on the farm. As with most farm kids, we didn't always have someone to entertain us, so we entertained ourselves. It was probably in our hideout under the elderberry bush on the hill behind the house that my older sisters (I was too young for these intellectual workouts) decided "Chris" was not a sufficient name for such a distinguished gentleman as Chris was, so his name was expanded to suit their fancies.

For the sake of the accuracy of this account, I recently e-mailed my older sisters about the full name of Chris, since I was young enough then that I wasn't sure I had it correct. The full name, according to Karen (the accepted authority on the subject), was "Christopher Columbus Alexander Daniel Boone Ferdinand deSoto Go-fetch-it Smith". He still answered when we called, "Here, Chris" so I don't know if he agreed with the full appellation or not.

It was a common thing in the society of the first half of the 1900s to use nicknames instead of a person's name, perhaps to show respect for names, perhaps to keep from forming close relationships, or sometimes to form close relationships. Also, most things around us were given nicknames, and Chris got called other things according to the current mindset of the family, most of all our dad's. One of his favorite names for Chris when things didn't go exactly right was a corruption of "Christopher" to "Pister."

I remember one morning when I was about five years old coming into the kitchen from my upstairs bedroom. Dad, Mother, and Chris were in the kitchen and as I said my good mornings to all, Chris seemed especially happy to see me, wagging his tail even more frantically than usual.

His tail was not cut short, as some bird dog tails are, but was over a foot long and had been injured early in life causing it to grow stiff and hard. He greeted me, turned away for Dad's approval of his greeting, and his club of a tail, still wagging, caught me between my five-year-old legs at just the wrong height. I shouted in pain, using dad's name for the dog, "Oh, Pister!" Needless to say, the event was the comic relief for that year—I remember even our enigmatic mother tucking in her chin and chuckling demurely to herself.

The significance of Chris and his name to me was demonstrated when I named my son after him. The residual power of the name was shown by my son, Chris, naming his son "Alexander" even though he had no inkling of that being part of the formal name of Old Chris. He still thinks I made up the story of the name, but it's all true. This seemed to be the beginning of my bird dogs influencing my life (and my posterity) in an unanticipated way.

Old Chris and the author, ca. 1945

Chapter 3
Tolerance

One of the difficult lessons of life is to learn tolerance, to put up with those who are different from us, or those who we think may have wronged us (whether they really did or not), or even someone who could, for whatever reason, be an enemy. This lesson was taught me as a boy by Old Chris.

Chris and I were in charge of pest control, and as soon as my arms were long enough to stabilize the barrel, Dad had me take the gun and Chris and I tried really hard to keep the rockchucks (marmots, groundhogs) out of the hay fields. It is amazing how a burrow in the rocks just outside the fence will supply enough chucks to trim all the useable hay in the field for at least a 50-foot circle from the entrance to the burrow. We would hunker down on the hill overlooking the field, and try our best to keep them out of the hay.

Rockchuck, or marmot (Photo courtesy of LeeAnn Gilbert)

One spring day Dad came home with his jacket wrapped around something and we gathered curiously to see what he had. Imagine our surprise when out popped two baby rockchucks, just big enough to get around. My sisters especially fell in love with them, and immediately took over the care and feeding of the orphans. The little chucks grew fast and made a home under the back porch.

You're getting ahead of me, but you're right—Chris instantly became their friend and protector, not letting any danger get near them. They would rub on him, play with his tail, otherwise be the kind of pests that playful youngsters can be, and Chris happily put up with it, for some years.

But this ruined him for his pest-control duties in the hayfield, right? Not at all—he fervently and happily went after the wild chucks that didn't belong, even though I suspect they smelled just like his friends, but he knew the difference. I learned that (1) no group should be condemned because of the actions of some of that group, and (2) the individual is apt to be desirable as a friend, given a fair chance, even though some who look much the same as him may not be.

Chapter 4
Better Than Christmas

I grew up in a home in Southern Idaho where, like in the great book, *A River Runs Through It,* "there was no clear line between religion and fly fishing." My dad was the kind of fly fisherman everybody wanted to fish with because he always caught fish. His favorite way of fishing was to send his guest along the river first, giving him the best chance at the unspooked trout, then Dad followed along behind and caught more and bigger fish than the visitor did, in the same spots and usually with the same fly. The guests went home shaking their heads in disbelief and leaving Dad chuckling.

I learned to fish before I could walk, according to my older sister. I do remember that there was no more important activity in my life, and my goal was to be as good at fishing as Dad was. Though I don't think I have achieved that, I'm still working on it. My favorite place as a toddler was the fish pond Dad had built below the spring west of the house. It was probably six or eight feet across, maybe twelve feet long, and had some big rocks at the edge where I could stand and watch the rainbow trout that dad had stocked there. The spring had a good flow of clear, cold water that kept the fish healthy, and there seemed to be plenty of food in the mossy swirls near the dark shadows of the big rocks. Occasionally a fat trout would swim out in the open where it could be seen, or surface to grab a bug or piece of bread thrown for the entertainment. This was fascinating to me to watch. Dad filed the barbs off a hook so we could do a version of catch-and-release, and taught me how to fish. I would have spent my life there, but Mother made me come in the house to eat and sleep.

When I was growing up, fishing season where we lived opened on the fourth of June. The timing of our life revolved around that date: the hay was cut starting June 5th, irrigation turns were scheduled so they could be managed with minimal effort—nothing was allowed to interfere with the most important day of the year. Most kids look forward to Christmas; I looked forward to June 4th—and still do—it's still like New Year's; life begins again on the fourth of June.

The author fishing, ca. 1943 (Photo courtesy Jean Nisson)

The point is, everyone needs something in their life that makes the heart do a flip, that generates some adrenalin, that is more exciting than the sometimes humdrum existence of go to work, eat, sleep, go to work, etc. Decide what gives your life some extra joy, then be sure to make time for that activity. Love life, live life, and look forward to the next day with enthusiasm for what's coming up.

Chapter 5
First Wild Fish

Since I had been schooled in technique at the spring pond, Dad figured I should try my luck at the true sport of fishing, trying to outsmart the wily wild trout. I was probably five or six years old when, on June 4th, opening day, Dad and I, just the two of us, walked down to the river below the island at the area which later became the family park. The river was in a different flow pattern then, with a deep hole and a shallow riffle and some exposed rocks above it, a perfect place for short legs and one even shorter on casting technique. Dad carried me piggy-back across the main channel to the rocks, set me down, made sure I had mastered letting the current carry my worm downstream to where the fish should be, then he slowly fished up river, watching me carefully.

Within what seemed like just a few minutes I had hooked and landed a rainbow trout, totally by myself, and to me it was the ultimate victory. Dad came back to share the excitement, so proud that his oldest son had mastered this most important technique. I don't know that anything in my life since has been more of a triumph.

My first fish seemed this big, but I know it wasn't.

Chapter 6
Don't Jump

When I was about five years old, a cousin, Keith Smith, some years older than I was, came to live with us for a few years. Since I had no older brothers, I instantly adopted him as a role model, a hero, a larger than life adventurer. I meant to do nothing that would diminish his stature in my eyes, or mine in his, as I imagined myself bigger and braver when he was around.
One of the daily chores of the small family farm is caring for the animals, including feeding the cows and horses, and in preparation for the coming winter we had stacked a summer's growth of alfalfa hay in the "stack yard" behind the barn, ready to be dished out, a pitchfork full at a time, twice a day. This haystack I remember to be one of the bigger ones, probably close to fifteen by twenty-five feet, and at least fifteen feet high. This was loose hay, not in bales. There was a long, homemade wooden ladder to get you on top of the stack to throw down hay for the animals. There were enough animals that throwing down the evening's feeding made quite a pile of hay next to the stack and those brave enough could jump off into space and land on the pile instead of climbing down the ladder, the safe way.

Of course, when Dad and Keith went out to feed, I followed along. They let me climb the ladder to the top of the stack, and after throwing down enough hay, Dad turned to me and said, "Now go down the ladder, don't you jump on the hay pile like we do, the stack is still too high." And they jumped off the stack to the top of the smaller pile, laughing and enjoying the thrill of free fall.

The mind of a young boy does not necessarily work logically or soundly, and especially does not use common sense. Since I had been told not to jump on the hay pile, I simply ran over to the corner of the stack opposite from where the hay had been thrown down, and jumped off. There was no thought of "there is no soft pile of hay to land on here, dummy" or anything else but "I'm going to jump just like they did." I landed on the frozen, hard ground, I cried, Dad and Keith came running around the stack, Keith gathered me up and carried me and my sprained ankle into the house. I remember hearing through my tears the two of them laughing at my stupidity, not believing that I would do such a dumb thing as to jump.

Chapter 7
The Loyalty of Old Chris

Growing up on a small farm in Southern Idaho we took advantage of the natural food sources around us. In season, there were pheasants, grouse, ducks, geese, and partridge, as well as deer and elk. The game birds were hunted most efficiently with a good bird dog, so Dad was very particular about having the right dog.

Old Chris was my tutor when I was young, up until my early teens. Chris was an exceptional hunter, and also a member of the family, and treated as one. None of us kids thought of him as a dog, he was like another brother, and he seemed to think he was, too—just a funny shaped kid. Where he did outshine us, and set an example for us, was in behavior. He had no dishonesty in his thinking, he obeyed without questioning, and he was totally loyal to Dad, his leader.

Probably the best example I remember of his loyalty was his devotion to hunting. He loved to hunt—the thrill of sniffing out, flushing and retrieving a bird was what he lived for. If he was not around when it was time to go hunting, all you had to do was step outside and work the action on the gun. Chris would magically appear, stiff stump of a tail wagging violently, tongue hanging out in anticipation of the fun to come. He followed the gun—wherever it went, he went, and he would leave it behind only to work a bird or retrieve one.

Chris would go with Dad when he was irrigating the hay fields, and would chase the ground squirrels that made holes in the ditch banks. Dad would sometimes carry a gun when he irrigated, to lessen the squirrel population when he could. One day when he returned from irrigating to have lunch we noticed that Chris was not with him. We thought he must be out sniffing around, as bird dogs do, but that evening he was still gone. That was really strange, as Chris valued his family time in the evenings. The next morning Chris was still missing. Now we were really worried, and discussed options as to where he might be. My sisters claim Chris was missing for a couple of days, but I think it was less than that, but either way it was really a significant amount of time.

As we sat somberly eating lunch, suddenly Dad said something under his breath that to my young ears sounded like a bad word, jumped up from the table, and headed out the door. Grabbing his shovel, he started up the hill toward the field where he had been irrigating the day (or was it two?) before.

After enough time had passed for him to change the irrigation water he returned, and with him was Old Chris. Dad explained that he had taken a gun with him when he went to irrigate, had leaned it on a fence post by the field, worked on the water and ditch, forgot the gun and came home. Chris, however, didn't forget the gun and stayed there by it, all day, all night, and until Dad finally showed up. He greeted Dad happily, hoping to go on a hunting trip, seemingly not caring even if he ate, as long as he was by the gun. His loyalty, it seemed, was endless. This was one of my early lessons in how to live, to be totally loyal to what you know you should be doing.

Chapter 8
Uncle Hebe

I was probably younger than six when old Uncle Hebe (Heber Walker, brother of my father's mother) died. I was too young to really be a part of his life, but so happy to have been able to consider that I was.

Uncle Hebe had lived in a shack just across the Bear River bridge by Uncle Lafe's house. Apparently it was truly a shack, a leftover from some earlier project, but to me it was where a favorite friend lived, so it was grand. I couldn't have been more than six years old when I began sneaking out with my fishing pole and heading for the river, crossing the bridge and asking Uncle Hebe if we could go fishing. I don't remember ever being turned down, but I do remember fishing with him in the spot we called, then and forever after, "Uncle Hebe's Hole." We would cross the county road and walk upstream through the willows along the bank on the south side of the river for maybe less than a hundred yards from the shack, then there was a small opening and a smooth, green, grassy spot that opened onto the river, right where the current formed a gentle eddy. This was "Uncle Hebe's Hole." It was fishable only when the river had the right flow—when the power plant a few miles upstream was running at just the right demand to create the proper current in the eddy and a depth that seemed to attract the fish into that "hole".

We would spend a few minutes on the way up the river catching grasshoppers along the bank and stuffing them into a Band-Aid can, then settle in on the grass, bait our hooks, and drift them along with the current, hoping to get the wily trout to bite.

I remember that nearly always we were successful, and I was so proud to have caught at least one before I heard Mother's frantic voice calling, "Dalan, where are you?"

It was always a mystery to me how she knew where to look for me, and Uncle Hebe always made me leave as soon as she showed up, even though my preference was to make one more cast.

My young mind didn't seem to comprehend the consternation that my regular disappearances caused my loving mother, not just because I went fishing without asking first, but also because of my choice of fishing partners. Uncle Hebe, to me, was a fine friend, a fishing pal, one who was always available on no advance notice, and who could catch a fish because he knew where to go. It was years later that I became enough acquainted with the ways of the world to realize how I would have felt as a parent had my son sneaked off with someone who spent his money and life on bottled goods, didn't seem to have much interest in working or getting ahead, and didn't care that he lived in sub-standard accommodations. I did know that his shack burned down not long after he passed away, but again it was years later that I finally heard the rumor that it was my dad that had set fire to it, to remove the attractive nuisance it had become.

Uncle Hebe's fishing hole

To me, Uncle Hebe continues to be one of my early heroes. It is still more important to me that he cared enough about a boy, not even his own, to share an activity that was really important to that small boy. I appreciate his friendship.

Chapter 9
Run!

When I was about six or seven years old, and my sister Karen was eleven or twelve, our main farm chore was bringing the cows home from the pastures at milking time. Neither of us really enjoyed this then like we would now, because it was a chore, not a reason for a pleasant walk over the hills. The cows ranged freely for a half-mile or so over the hillsides and hollows of the farm to find feed, and we never knew exactly where they would be. The only thing we seemed to be sure of was that they would be in the most unexpected or hardest to reach places. Maybe this attitude was what made us delay as long as possible in going to get them, or perhaps it was just that secretly we thought if we delayed long enough they would come in by themselves or Dad would give up on us and go get them.

One evening we found a reason to delay longer than we should have, and it was nearly dark before we started out. The cows weren't on the lower hills, they weren't by the hay field, we didn't find them in Big Hollow, so they must be in First Hollow, and we had to trek to that more remote area. By now it was dark, and we followed a narrow trail through the sagebrush up the bottom of the hollow. This was strange country to us, as we didn't get there often. It was far from the house, and always seemed spooky. Owls lived there and who knew what else lurked where the sage gave way to a small grove of cottonwood trees and willows that made dark shapes against the faint light of the sky. The stars were out, but no "cow shapes" showed up anywhere.

We followed the trail up the hollow almost to the grove of trees, stopped to decide where to go next, and as we stood in the dark by a large sage bush suddenly there was a loud buzzing sound near us. We stood motionless a moment, not knowing what it was, then Karen yelled, "Rattlesnake, <u>run</u>!"

Instantly she was gone, disappearing down the hollow on the trail we had just traveled. Now, the term "trail" is misleading, for it was actually little more than a faint track through the sagebrush, and to follow it in the daylight is not easy, but in the dark on a dead run was impossible. I ran, I cried, my eyes filled with tears and not only was it dark, but I couldn't see even if it was not. I tripped and fell down, got up, ran some more, Karen was missing and maybe the snake got her. I was alone in the dark and I was sure the snake was slithering rapidly down the trail behind me, coming to get me too. I alternately ran, stumbled, fell, got up and ran some more, all the way home. When I finally got there, the cows had shown up by themselves and Dad was milking. Karen was in the warm, bright kitchen telling Mother about our harrowing experience, and I felt a little silly, having run so much and so far that all my fears and tears had dissolved.

Chapter 10
Chris' Wild Goose Chase

Old Chris would retrieve anything that we hunted. Of course, he was not invited on big-game hunts (and he understood, it seems, for he would not ever show more than a passing interest in, let alone chase, a deer), but bird hunting was not complete, or even enjoyable, without him to sniff out and fetch the pheasants, ducks, or geese.

There were not many geese that frequented the little valley along the Bear River where we lived, so we sometimes traveled to the Blackfoot Reservoir above Soda Springs to get a chance at putting a goose in our freezer. I was around ten years old one year that we hunted there, too young to hunt, but an eager spectator. As dawn came, we hunkered down on a ridge between two bays of the reservoir and waited for the geese to fly over in shotgun range. The spot was well-chosen, for soon flocks of geese started flying out to feed on the surrounding grain fields, most too high to shoot at effectively. Soon we heard a lone "honk" from a straggler, and sure enough, this one was in range.

Blackfoot Reservoir

Dad's shot was not as good as it could have been, and the goose came down with just a damaged wing, landing near the edge of the water. Old Chris ran full speed down the hill, vaulting over the sagebrush, intent on retrieving the goose. As he reached the beach, the goose saw him coming and began to swim toward the center of the lake to safety. This was no obstacle to Chris, for he was a powerful swimmer, and he loved the water. The problem, however, that Chris hadn't figured out yet, was that a full-grown goose can swim faster than any dog. Besides that, a goose floats whether it is paddling or not, but a dog floats only when its feet are moving.

Chris swam after the fleeing goose. The Blackfoot Reservoir is huge, miles across, and is a really safe place for a goose. It is not a safe place for something that doesn't float — like a bird dog. We ran down to the water's edge and called to Chris to give up the chase, but he was determined to catch and retrieve that goose; that was his job. They swam until they were no more than two dots on the water, the goose getting further and further ahead. Dad cussed, figuring Chris had gone beyond the point of no return, that he surely couldn't make it back to shore from that far out. All we could do was sit down and wait. It seemed like an eternity, waiting for something to happen, perhaps for Dad to say, "Well, let's go home, Chris had a good life, and left it doing what he loved best."

Then, unexpectedly, one of the dots reappeared and started getting bigger. Chris had realized his limits and turned around. We jumped to our feet and cheered, urging him to keep paddling, knowing he still was in real danger so far from the safety of land. Did he have enough stamina to continue that far?

No sports figure has had a more loyal fan club, and maybe that helped keep his spirits up. We cheered, he paddled, we cheered more, he got closer, finally his big feet touched the sand and he staggered up to us, then collapsed in a soggy heap, tongue hanging out and panting rapidly. He had made it. We happily went home with no geese, the day a complete success.

I think sometimes of this lesson in knowing our limits, and thank Old Chris again.

Chapter 11
Salmon River, East Fork Camp

Some of the fondest memories of my youth center around fishing trips, and none were of more import to my fishing-addicted self than those to the Salmon River country of central Idaho. To be able to add to the family larders several pounds of fresh salmon was a remarkable blessing, to say nothing of the recreation of the trip and the catch. I still marvel that those fish, seeking a spawning ground, swim up the Columbia River out of the Pacific Ocean, enter the Snake River near Kennewick, Washington, travel up the Snake River past Lewiston, Idaho, and then make their way upstream in the Salmon River and its tributaries to destinations near where they were hatched some years earlier. All the energy for this trip comes from stored reserves, as they won't eat once they enter the river systems on this end-of-life journey.

My earliest memories of the Salmon River trips involved riding with Uncle Hyrum in the big Nash automobiles he drove. We usually left home in the early evening and traveled all night, arriving at our destination on the Salmon River about daylight the next morning, just in time to start fishing. Although I was too little to fish for salmon, I loved those trips. My dad had taught me how to find the direction we were traveling from looking at the stars, and I would marvel how the stars changed positions in the car windows all during the night, how my head didn't keep up with which way we were going while I was asleep, and I would have to reorient myself each time I woke and looked up at the sky.

My favorite camping spot was on the East Fork of the Salmon River, just below a bridge, on the banks overlooking a deep hole of slow-moving water where the salmon would rest for a time before moving on up the river. At the outflow of this hole was a wide, shallow riffle that dropped sharply into the river below and made a distinct rushing sound all day and night. It was a wonderful lullaby sound to sleep to.

There was an established camping spot where we pitched tents and built a cooking fire, near enough to the road that the cars could park there, yet only steps from the river. The bridge, just upstream from the camping place, provided easy access to either side of the river, to allow fishing at the best angles according to the time of day. Although I didn't feel safe fishing for salmon, I loved to fish for the trout that also lived in the East Fork.

I remember distinctly one afternoon crossing the river bridge and positioning myself on the cliff overlooking the deep hole to fish for trout. I had fished for a while with no luck, when suddenly, right in front of me, not more than fifteen feet away, a large salmon reared out of the water, shook its light-brown colored body in the air, and dropped back into the water just feet from where my line and lure were positioned. I was so startled, and my system so filled with adrenaline, that I could picture this giant of a fish getting on the end of my line and pulling me into the river from my precarious perch on top of the cliff I was on. I wanted nothing to do with that, so I pulled up my line, climbed up the bank, ran across the bridge and down to the camp to excitedly report that there was a salmon in the deep hole, just waiting to be caught. No, we didn't catch it, except in my mind, where the picture will resonate forever. Dad, my uncles, and the cousins that went with us did catch some salmon, and the trip was a success.

Chapter 12
Old Sinner

Cousin Theo Smith and his wife, Arda, lived across Bear River from us while I was growing up. Because the river was too big to wade when the water was high, I always felt Theo had a corner on the fishing on that side, and I dearly wished I could fish there. Reaching as far as I could cast from our side of the stream didn't do it. My 12-year-old brain figured out that if I could ride my bike over the bridge which was just up the river, then I wouldn't have to do such a long walk to get there, try the fishing, and get back home.

There was an obstacle to this plan—his name was "Old Sinner," a curly-haired bird dog (I think a Chesapeake Retriever) that defended his territory fiercely against all who intruded, and was big enough to see that nobody challenged his authority. After a time, I figured out a plan. The security officer, Old Sinner, was too mean to run loose, so he was kept chained to the barn whenever Theo was out in the fields or otherwise away from home. The chain was short enough so I could skinny past down the lane on my bike, and then the farm lane ran all the way to the fishing hole. A dog on the end of a chain is safe, no matter how loud he barks, right?

The plan worked. I found a time when Theo was off the premises, zipped down the lane past the barking dog and spent a couple of hours fishing. When it was time to go home, I pedaled nonchalantly up the lane, heard the barking begin and pedaled on, confident in the safety the chain provided. One unforeseen action tripped up the good plan—Theo had come in for lunch and unhooked Old Sinner's chain for a little exercise, having no idea somebody else was around. After all, I hadn't bothered to tell anyone I was there.

The ferocious barking seemed louder this time, and I looked toward the barn just as a brown, curly haired, huge, growling, ferocious owner of a set of big teeth launched himself through the air and landed tooth-first on my leg. I was sure I was destined for death in a couple of moments, but Theo came out of the house to see what was going on and pulled off his security guard. Old Sinner had punched a deep hole in my right leg just below the knee. He chained the dog, gave me a ride home and apologized to my mother. No need to, the dog was just doing his job—I'm the one who was in the wrong by not asking permission to go down the lane so the dog could be kept chained up. I healed okay, grew up in spite of Old Sinner, and realized later it was probably my fault he disappeared shortly after that incident.

Chapter 13
Dad's Snake

One of the chores of taking care of the Twin Lakes Canal was cleaning the screen that was above the siphon crossing Bear River. Dad seemed to be the one who spent more time at this than anyone else, and sometimes I got to go watch, climbing the zig-zag trail up the hill on the other side of the river to the head of the siphon, where a spillway took excess water down the hill into the river. There was a wooden headgate bridge that spanned the canal where I could even occasionally help move sticks that had floated down and lodged on the bars of the screen, using a long pole with a two-pronged hook to balance them until they could be reached and discarded on a pile to be burned later.

I vividly remember going with dad to do this chore one spring day when I was probably six years old or so. It seemed hotter than usual for early morning, and the hill seemed steeper, and when we reached the top I was too tired to badger dad about helping him, so I went to the bridge across the spillway to rest while he cleaned the screen. Two of my older sisters were with us, as we were going to make a day of it, going on down to the Mink Creek place where we had some hay fields and a stackyard.

Dad was cleaning the screen, standing on a pile of brush that had been moved out of the canal, when he realized a stick or something kept hitting his heavy rubber boot. He looked down and with horror realized it was a rattlesnake, striking him repeatedly as it was apparently trapped by the brush he was standing on.

In order to really appreciate this situation, the reader must understand the long-standing fear of snakes in the Smith family, almost legendary in its magnitude. Dad had inherited this characteristic, and his heart leaped at knowing one of the most-feared creatures of his imagination not only existed, but was trying its best to bite him. The pole being used to clean the screen came into play immediately, and when Dad stopped swinging it, the snake was little more than a grease spot on the brush. He immediately said that was enough cleaning, we would head for the hayfields.

As we went down the hill on the Mink Creek side Dad was visibly shaken, but he was so happy the heavy rubber boots had kept the fangs from reaching his leg, and was determined to finish the day's work.

We crossed the hay fields and went to the stackyard near the Mink Creek road to get the derrick ready for the season of haying. Each fall the long pole that lifted the hay to the stack was let down to the ground, and each spring it had to be put up again. To do this, Dad ran a cable under one of the logs that formed the base and then used a tractor to pull the pole into place. He pushed the cable under the log, then reached from the near side to hook it with his finger and pull it through to attach to the chain from the tractor. As he pulled the cable under the log, it didn't feel just right, and he looked down to see he had hooked with his finger the body of another snake, one with patterns like a rattlesnake, and was pulling it out from under the log. Now reflexes took over, as he was still keyed up from his near-bite experience at the screen, and his arm continued its pull, accelerating rapidly, and he ripped the snake out from under the log and continued the upward motion until the snake was flying through the air, end over end, and probably still is. Dad stood up, shook himself, and said, "We're going home!" and headed for the road. My short legs could hardly keep up, and my sisters grabbed me from either side to keep me going on a near run.

In retrospect, Dad realized that the second snake was a blow snake (gopher snake) not a rattler, but it didn't matter, the adrenaline was flowing, and the snake got a huge lift. The experience of that day, taken as a whole, was added to the legends of the Smith fear of snakes, and became one of our favorite stories.

Chapter 14
Enthusiasm, Used and Misused

Life can be so much fun, so enjoyable, if we can just keep our enthusiasm in the right vein. It can make a dreary, hum-drum job a pleasurable experience, and can cement a relationship with a friend to a degree we never dreamed possible. On the other hand, if channeled improperly, enthusiasm can cause us and those around us severe pain and/or embarrassment.

One of my favorite pleasures in life is fly-fishing. A particular stream always brought my enthusiasm up more than others. One bend in the creek seemed to hold a ready supply of 12-inch cutthroat trout with a peculiar characteristic that I've seldom experienced anywhere else. I sneaked up behind the small willows on the bank and threw my fly to the head of the riffle so it could float down through the hole to where the trout should feed. On the first cast, and before the fly had floated to where I thought the fish would be, an over-enthusiastic trout launched itself at my fly, catching it on the way up, and sailed right out of the water, through the air for a foot or more, then headed for the bottom of the fishing hole. When it happened, I was so surprised I nearly missed catching the fish, but reflexes took over and automatically set the hook at the right time.

The next year I went to that spot first, remembering the fun from the year before of catching and releasing that beautiful, super-active fish, and was completely surprised when the identical thing took place. The fish sailed up out of the water with my hook in its mouth, and again reflexes took charge. I was so startled that after I released the fish, I broke out laughing—standing alone on the bank of the creek shaking my head, laughing out loud and looking, I'm sure, like a complete idiot in my enthusiasm, and not even caring.

On the other hand, the uncontrolled enthusiasm of one party in a situation can ruin the day for the others. When I was growing up, Dad and I used to look forward with great anticipation to the opening day of pheasant season. One of our neighbors, John Youngman, not really a hunter, asked us to hunt with him on the opening day because he had a new bird dog he wanted to use. We of course were skeptical of the training, if any, of this mighty Chesapeake Retriever, but consented to hunt with John anyway, partly because we had always seen ample pheasants on John's farm and usually didn't get to hunt there.

The season always opened at noon on the first day, and when we arrived at John's place a little before that, he was standing in the yard with a really long face. He explained that a little earlier his dog had decided what "opening day" meant, and had started enthusiastically hunting through the fields. By the time we arrived, all the pheasants had been flushed, had sailed across the river and landed high on a big sagebrush-covered hill, impossible to hunt successfully. So much for the pheasant hunt, so much for the new dog, and so much for out-of-control enthusiasm.

Chapter 15
Favorite Holiday

Perhaps it is because I remember the fondness with which my dad referred to Groundhog Day that this has become my favorite holiday. It is not necessary for the world to celebrate together with a day off work, or businesses closed, or calendars to have a different color for a day to be recognized as a holiday, but only for it to be special in the mind of the one doing the celebrating, and in my mind Groundhog Day will always be special.

I remember my father always wondering, and sometimes walking over the hills on our farm looking eagerly around for signs that would indicate a groundhog (or rock chuck, as we called the fat rodents) had been out and would have a chance to see his shadow, or not. Early February in southeastern Idaho is not exactly spring, even in the warmest of years, and often the snow was still deep, the burrows of the animals covered with a white blanket. I didn't understand why father thought these guys would be out and about, as opposed to still curled up and slumbering in that cozy state of hibernation where they passed the winter. Also, I couldn't fathom what a rock chuck had to say about the weather and its prognostication, anyway! It was years later that I adopted my own philosophy about weather watching, and it became a favorite pastime. Now, as February second approaches, I, just as eagerly as Dad did, tend to look around and hope to glimpse a furry body soaking up a little of the sunshine that may or may not have a tinge of spring in it.

It's not as if these animals were our favorite friends, for they were quite a pest in the fields near their burrows, as they would feed happily on new alfalfa or growing stalks of grain crops. In fact, their control was one of my earliest farm duties, and our bird dog Chris and I would spend hours sitting on the hill waiting for one to appear from underground and make a target in my sights. Funny, we could never seem to eliminate all of them; it was as if their destiny was to provide some opposition to healthy crops, or at least to serve as a reason for me to spend time guarding the fields. Remember there were those two rock chucks that were special to us, those that had a burrow under the back porch to the house where we lived? They adopted our family home as theirs and lived there for years, completely at home with us, including Chris and I, mortal enemies of their field-dwelling cousins though we were. It was a lesson in life for me as I grew up to remember to not automatically attach a label to any group for any reason, as some of the group may have some redeeming features, after all.

Every year the show "Groundhog Day" is on television again, and it has some interesting philosophies. If you haven't watched it recently, I recommend you look at it with an eye to learning some life lessons. No doubt there is some merit to the idea that it is really desirable to reach a certain level of performance before we are ready to move on. Think about it.

THE "BUTCH" ERA

Chapter 16
Patience Has Its Rewards

Keeping entertained as a teenager on a small farm in southern Idaho in the 1950s was a far cry from what we see teens do now to keep themselves occupied. A favorite entertainment for my brothers and me during hunting season was jump-shooting ducks on the Twin Lakes Canal that ran around the hillsides of the farm. The ducks liked to feed on the grain fields near the canal then go to the water for a cool, comforting swim. We learned that this was an excellent time to sneak up and get some ducks for supper.

The most effective method of hunting was jump-shooting, which seemed simple, but required following a few basic rules. The cardinal rule was not to let the wary ducks see you before you were in shotgun range, or they were instantly gone. We would look far ahead to locate where the ducks were swimming, then go down over the lower bank and travel, out of sight, until we were near enough to them to come up over the bank and get a shot. Sometimes the quarry would see our movement when we spotted them, and travel quietly the other direction, so we would have to do another sneak to get in range. This strategy is quite understandable to humans, but to a bird dog the headfirst charge, regardless of the distance, seems the most desirable. Training the dog to follow down over the bank and to stay at my heels until the gun went off was sometimes a nearly impossible task. The energy of genetics, the inborn instinct to hunt, flush, and retrieve is so strong that some dogs never have the self-mastery to resist running after the quarry too early. For those that did learn the proper method, the reward to both the hunter and the dog is a great satisfaction.

The master of the "canal sneak" was Butch. Perhaps it was his water spaniel breeding that influenced this. He loved hunting ducks, would follow obediently during the sneak, and never missed seeing where every duck fell, retrieving sometimes two at once. If one was floating down with the current, Butch would launch off the top of the bank, sail through the air, land with a mighty splash and come up swimming strongly in the right direction, or sometimes even with the duck already in his mouth. The successful retrieve was his reward, and he lived for a pat and congratulatory thank you for each one, needing no more pay than that. No bank was too high to jump off, and if on the return the bank was too steep to climb he would swim up or downstream to where he could clamor up to complete his retrieve. He trained both my younger brothers to hunt, and was a faithful escort whenever needed. As with other lessons, I think I learned more from him about discipline and reserving my energies for that which is most important than he did on any subject from me.

Duck on a canal

Chapter 17
Butch's High-Speed Adventure

Dad did most of his driving in a 1948 Ford pickup that was the farm truck, and Butch loved riding in the back. Around the farm or close to home he was never tied up, but when he went the ten miles or so to Preston dad felt more secure with him tied in the back of the truck, to prevent Butch from chasing any of the new sights, sounds, or smells that he encountered.

One day apparently Dad was in a hurry, or somehow distracted, and tied Butch's rope to the side of the truck bed instead of the center. I'm sure it never occurred to him that this may result in a problem, and was driving along when someone pulled up alongside waving frantically and gesturing to the rear. Dad looked in the mirror and saw, to his horror, Butch outside the truck, still tethered, keeping upright at 40 miles an hour by jumping in the air, landing and jumping, landing and jumping…

When dad pulled over and inspected Butch for damage, he found the pads of his paws were pretty well skidded off, but no other problems. He picked Butch up and put him in the cab of the truck, and completed his trip. Butch was sore for a few days, but healed completely. Since that time I have been ultra-conscious of the potential for damage to animals and others that may have occasion to be tethered to something, whether physically or otherwise.

Chapter 18
Gradual Growth

We're often hearing that our lives develop "line upon line" as we gain knowledge or ability, whether it is in temporal or spiritual things. When I was young, my dad taught this principle to us in a unique way, by taking us to the Greys River near Star Valley, Wyoming.

The Greys River flows through Alpine, Wyoming, coming from the mountains to the southeast of Alpine to meet the South Fork of the Snake River that runs down the Grand Canyon of the Snake from Jackson Hole. It is a mountain river of reasonable size at that point, with good fishing and enough water to kayak or float in a raft.

To show us the lesson in gradual growth, dad turned off Highway 89 (coming from Idaho) before we dropped into the south end of Star Valley. We traveled east on a forest road across ridge tops, viewing wildlife and spectacular scenery. Finally dad said, "Look at the little trickle of water from those springs, that is the beginning of the Greys River." I was really annoyed that we had traveled for a few hours and now had come to a stream too small to fish in, but dad suggested I be a little more patient, there was still something to see. The road headed generally north from there on, and every now and then dad would say, "See, it's bigger." Apparently I wasn't paying attention, because it still looked to me to be too puny for any fishing and I had not seen any tributaries of any significance adding to the flow. I was becoming quite bored with this, in spite of his enthusiasm and obvious love for the river and the surrounding forest.

We were traveling down a growing canyon, and when dad pulled off into a parking spot, suddenly I realized there was fishable water. Now I was excited. We fished, caught some native cutthroat trout and some whitefish, then traveled downstream some more, stopping occasionally to fish. As the miles passed, the river grew markedly, with growing rapids, wide open stretches, and plenty of water.

It finally occurred to me what dad was trying to teach me. Life is like the Greys River, he had said, and now I began to see some sense in his words, for I realized that our growth is sometimes almost imperceptible. The knowledge, skills, or abilities we obtain may not be evident at first, but when the need arises to perform on a higher level than ever before, we can do it because of that often imperceptible but very persistent and effective growth.

Some scenery at the head of the Greys River

Chapter 19
Night Wanderer

Butch was a great bird dog, a really good family friend, lots of company if you were alone with him, and he never offered to be mean to anyone. If he had a fault, it was that as a young male dog he seemed to have an overabundance of hormones.

I remember Dad complaining about Butch going visiting at night, and not knowing where he went. Now and then he would show signs of having been in a fight with another dog, and Dad was worried he might get really hurt. This went on for quite some time, until one early morning Dad was headed up the road to Mink Creek and near where Hugh Hansen lived, about a mile away from home, he found Butch. Butch was just sitting there, right in the middle of the county road, not seeming to care if he was alive or about to be run over. He was pretty beat up, with some bloody spots, and looked really discouraged, as if he had not only lost the fight physically, but also had lost all his inner ability to fight. Dad put him in the truck and brought him home, mumbling something about a change of attitude. I was a young teenager then, and not very knowledgeable about a lot of things, but being raised on a farm you can't help but learn some basics, and I was about to get a lesson about hormone production.

Dad was a long time farmer, with a lot of animal doctoring experience and not a lot of money to pay for veterinarians, so most things he did himself, including gelding horses and castrating calves (or dogs). He instructed me to bring an old coat to wrap Butch in, legs and all, to restrain him, and especially to cover his mouth so he couldn't bite anyone if it hurt too bad.

Then I knew what was about to happen, and felt sorry for Butch, but his wandering ways had earned him what he was going to get. With deft fingers, Dad took care of the operation while I held Butch securely, and then we turned him loose to heal. Heal he did, and from then on he stayed home at night, didn't fight any more, had a really nice attitude about most everything, and best of all remained a great bird dog. More than once in my life, as I have met human males with an attitude similar to that which the youngster Butch had, it has crossed my mind that a similar attitude adjustment is needed. It is a blessing to know we can grow out of those overactive ways without resorting to surgery.

Chapter 20
Smells Like Gas in Here!

When I was probably 14 or 15 I had a Tote Goat scooter that I loved to ride to the river to fish. It saved much time, and was a lot easier than walking. I got pretty good at balancing my fishing pole and still keeping control of the scooter. The problem I had was there was never enough gasoline in the tank. Living almost ten miles out of town as we did precluded a quick trip to the gas station, so we had to be very creative in filling the tank.

One morning I really wanted to go fishing, so I got a siphon hose and a gas can and headed for the tractor. Living on a small farm demands that you take advantage of all the resources around you, and a tractor with gas in the tank is an opportunity that even Dad would understand, so I didn't fear any repercussions. I dropped the end of the hose into the tank on the tractor, held the other end close to the gas can and gave a big suck on the hose to get the siphon action started. Apparently I forgot that the fuel tank on the tractor was up high, and any liquid runs downhill, and especially one as liquid as gasoline runs downhill very fast. My mouth filled with gas, an involuntary swallowing action took place, and it tasted awful. I must have swallowed a tablespoon full or more of gasoline. The good part was the siphon hose was running, the gas can was filling, and after lunch I could go fishing.

Soon lunch was ready, so we sat down at the table. My younger brother, Norman, was sitting next to me, as always, and all went well until I burped. Right after the burp (which tasted like the inside of a refinery) Norman said, "I smell gas!" I ignored him, and went on eating lunch.

My system kept objecting to the contents of my stomach, and I kept burping. Each time I exhaled, Norman exclaimed, "I smell gas!" Our parents must have thought I had spilled some on my clothes or hands, for they never questioned us any further. After lunch I went fishing, and gradually the smelly burps went away. I learned that time can heal even the most obvious problems.

Chapter 21
The Last Old-fashioned Haystack

Our small farm in Southern Idaho was one of the last pretty much self-sufficient old-time family farms with acreage for growing grain to sell and hay for the few milk cows, some egg-laying chickens, sometimes a pig or two, a granary for storing the grain, and a stackyard by the milk barn for storing a crop of hay to get the livestock through the winter. This stackyard was fenced securely and had mangers along part of two or three sides to make it convenient to put hay in that the cattle could reach through and eat. Nobody we knew had a hay baler yet, so the hay was put up loose.

The hay was mostly alfalfa, as this had a good protein content, good fiber, and if cut and cured properly was an excellent feed. The cutting was done when the plants first started to bloom, as this was the time of optimum feed value. The first hay I remember working with was cut with a horse-drawn mower, a very slow process compared to today's mechanized equipment. After the hay was left to cure in the open air for a couple of days, depending on the weather, a dump rake (also horse-drawn) was used to rake it into windrows, then came the fun part of pulling the rake along the windrow to make individual piles ready to be hauled. These were loaded by pitchfork onto a hay rack. It was my job as a youngster to tromp the hay firmly onto the rack to allow a maximum weight load, and also to make it stable so not to slide around on the way down the hill to the stackyard.

Dominating the stackyard was the derrick pole (actually the full trunk of a sizeable pine tree) set at an angle so it could pivot on a shorter, upright pole on a log base. The derrick pole had a pulley on the upper end, and there was one at the top and bottom of the upright. Through these pulleys ran a strong cable which attached to the harness of a horse (the derrick horse) and on the other end to a wonderful thing called a Jackson Fork. This had four tines, each about three feet long, and set about a foot apart on a wooden frame. There is an ingenious latch that when engaged holds the curved tines so they hook into the hay when the derrick horse takes up the cable, so the hay is lifted off the rack and into the air. Obviously, this requires one man on the hay rack to set the fork into the hay, one on the derrick horse to direct it, and one on the stack to place each load properly. When the fork full of hay is pulled up higher than the stack, the derrick horse is stopped, the pole swivels until the hay is in the proper place, then the stacker yells, "Let 'er go!" and the rope is pulled to release the latch and dump the fork full of hay onto the stack. The horse then backs up, lowering the fork to start the cycle again.

    Building a proper stack is truly an art that is almost lost in this day of balers, choppers, and silage sacks. "Progress" seems to have no compunction about replacing old things until they disappear forever. How grateful we are that there are historical farms that maintain some of these arts, not just so we can remember how to do those things, but also to remind us of how hard those before us worked.

The last haystack, August 1959

Chapter 22
Clarabelle and a Shady Tree

Dad grew up in the days when cars were scarce, and spent much time in the saddle. He was a good rider and enjoyed riding, especially with family. When I was in my early teens we only had one saddle horse, Wimpy, and one of the neighbors had given us a burro, Clarabelle, to take care of. We had an old army saddle (McClellan style) and found it fit Clarabelle pretty well, at least good enough to use, so Dad thought we should go riding together.

Clarabelle and Dad, 1958

It was a bright, sunny, hot July day. Clarabelle accepted the saddle, so we saddled the horse as well, and off we went. We rode up the Bear River Narrows road to Cave Mountain, and then turned up the Maple Canyons road.

By this time we were pretty warm, but still enjoying, as we hadn't ridden in a while. The humans were nice and warm, but our mounts were sweating and looking really warm, and we weren't sure they were enjoying the trip as much as we were.

After about half a mile of traveling up hill on the side road we were passing a lone cedar tree not far off the road. It cast a nice shadow, and as we were about to ride by it, suddenly Clarabelle turned and started toward the tree. Dad pulled on the reins, kicked, yelled at her, and only succeeded in making her go faster toward the tree. Nothing he could do would change her direction. When she reached the tree she veered into the shade, put her head down, and, planting her front hooves firmly in the soil stopped so suddenly that Dad went right over her head and landed on a sage bush.

Clarabelle didn't even look at him, just calmly stood there in the shade, cooling off. Dad gathered himself up and started toward the road, to lead the burro back there and get on again. This worked fine until he got to the end of the reins, and realized she was not following him and was not going to follow him, but was happy there in the shade. Nothing he did would get her to move into the sunshine. He discussed this lack of cooperation with her at length, using some very descriptive wording and phraseology, but she didn't seem to hear any of it, and certainly wasn't going to follow him anywhere at the moment. Dad wasn't dumb, did have a great sense of humor, and as he realized who was in control of the situation, began to chuckle, and sitting down in the shade beside the new trail boss said, "Why don't we rest in the shade a few minutes?"

It only took a few minutes for Clarabelle to cool off and catch her breath, then she let Dad get on again and we went up the road. We learned that as soon as she was too hot or getting tired Clarabelle would call for a rest, and we learned that under those long, funny-looking ears was some common sense. From then on anytime Dad suggested I had less sense than a jackass I knew exactly who he was referring to.

Chapter 23
Meadow Creek

One of my favorite fishing days of all time took place on Meadow Creek, a feeder stream of the Blackfoot Reservoir. Dad and I, and someone else, I don't remember who, had gone to the Blackfoot Reservoir in search of the huge trout that lived there, but had arrived about a half an hour too late. There was a period of an hour or so right about daylight when the fish would bite, then they seemed to disappear for the rest of the day, and we got there right after that. Some other fishermen had camped overnight and had been in place for the feeding frenzy, and showed us two trout in the seven or eight pound range that they had just caught. We were sick that we had missed out. It took our enthusiasm away for fishing, but we went through the motions, anyway, and sure enough, caught nothing.

It wasn't too long before Dad said, "I like stream fishing better, let's go see if we can find a fish in Meadow Creek." We packed up and headed up the road.

Meadow Creek below the meadows

Meadow Creek is just what its name suggests, a small stream that meanders for miles through a large, nearly level meadow before it drops through some foothills into the reservoir. On these upper reaches it is winding, generally quite slow moving, and has some deeper holes as well as some shallow, mossy spots. We parked at the bridge and Dad said, "I'd like to fish downstream, what about you?" I chose to go upstream, and our friend, who was somewhat of a novice, decided to tag along with Dad. I climbed through the fence and walked a ways looking for a good place to fish. It is always more of a pleasure to fish alone, at my own pace, when I can get in the spirit of the activity with no interruptions for conversation or interactions with anyone but the stream and the fish.

I found some places, caught a couple of small trout, and then spied a really likely-looking hole, a spot of dark, deep water in between two pillars of moss, not very wide, but definitely promising. I was using a small, double spinner, and as it swung through the hole a large, brown back appeared from the depths and followed the spinner across near the surface, then disappeared into the dark water again. I was so startled I pulled my lure from the water and just stood there a few moments, trying to decide what the best course of action was now that I knew where there was a really nice trout. I backed slowly and carefully away from the stream to think about it.

My schooling in the stalking of the wily trout had included many lessons on how to keep from spooking fish, and I brought them all into play now. The stream was small — no, tiny — and any quick moves or harsh steps could create vibrations that would warn the trout of danger. I slowly and carefully moved out into the meadow away from the stream, then went back downstream to think.

There was nobody else around, so I was safe that way, but it was the bright time of the day, the sun was shining, and would the spinner I had been using be too much? Is that why the trout had looked, but didn't bite? Would there be another lure that would be better? What would bring him up from the depths again? Would it be better to wait longer?

After spending some time on these weighty matters, I decided that I should act now, and that the same lure would give me the best chance, so I crept back to the hole, squatting down and sneaking up on it as if I were stalking something extraordinary, as I indeed was. I knew I had no margin for error in placing the lure in the water to get it to move over the place I had seen the trout, and I took extra time to make certain it was exact. The spinner slipped gently into the water, I let it sink a little, then brought it to life with a smooth, gentle pull. It had hardly begun to move when that large, brown back appeared again, this time moving directly toward my lure. This is when many fishermen fail, when they react too soon and spook the fish before the bite, but my schooling was good, and I let the fish swim right up to the spinner. It bit, I set the hook, and it took just a few moments to land the fish in the small stream. I was elated—in my wildest daydreams I hadn't conjured up a three-pound trout in the tiny stream called Meadow Creek, but here it was in all reality.

When we met some time later at the car, Dad (my instructor) asked if I had done any good and I told him I felt I had followed his teachings very well, thank you, and pulled from my creel the two small trout. He beamed that I had caught some, and then I reached in again and brought out the real prize. His jaw dropped, he laughed out loud, and stood there in disbelief, just shaking his head. He had caught some small ones, also, but that was all. The lesson of Meadow Creek was that if the instructions are followed, the results will come.

Chapter 24
A Real Good Hunting Horse

As I was growing up, family finances were tight, and hunting was heavily relied on to provide meat for the winter. The real prize was an elk, both in quality of meat and in quantity, so elk hunting was a serious business each fall. There were very few of those animals near the farm, so travel was usually involved. One year Dad traveled with two of my older cousins, Dean and Theo Smith, to Fremont County, near Ashton, Idaho, thinking there was a good chance to find elk there. It just wasn't to be, and they started home, but took a last minute detour to Swan Valley, knowing that was also a good area for elk. They were hauling horses in a stock truck, knowing they could cover more ground on a horse than on foot, and also would have horses to pack out meat if the hunt was successful.

In Swan Valley, they split up to search as much country as possible, with Dad electing to go up high on the mountain on one of the cousins' old cow horses, and the cousins hunting the lower quaking aspen breaks. Dad had gone miles with no sign of game and had nearly circled back to the truck when suddenly a herd of elk appeared just across a meadow, but out of rifle range. They saw him and took off, so he kicked the horse in the ribs and headed down the other side of a strip of timber from the elk, but in the same general direction. In a matter of a few hundred yards, the trees tapered down to meadow again.

As Dad and the galloping horse came to the end of the timber, the elk, also on the run down the other side of the trees, suddenly were running right alongside them through the meadow. The old cow horse decided it was a roundup, this was really fun, and sped up to match the speed of the elk. Dad was frantically pulling on the reins and talking to the horse, so he could get off and shoot, but the horse was not listening. Seeing it was no use to try to steer or stop, Dad threw his feet out of the stirrups and rolled off the back of the horse. He landed on his back, rolled to a sitting position and with the gun braced between his knees, collected our winter meat. As the remaining elk disappeared over the hill, the good old cow horse realized the roundup was out of control and stopped. He and Dad were both satisfied.

As dad told us the story later, I realized some control and discretion must apply to all exciting situations. The horse's ignoring Dad's orders to stop could have been a serious problem had Dad been injured getting off. The instinctive running to head off the herd should have still been subject to some direction from the rider, but it is so difficult when the adrenaline is flowing to remember that, even for an old cow horse.

Chapter 25
Avoid the Very Appearance of Danger,
Or Operating on the Edge

My brothers and I got a huge amount of our entertainment from Butch. Not only was he a super bird dog for hunting, but off-season he would fetch sticks thrown in the river, would go with us on any hike, visits to the neighbors, or chores around the farm—was just great company for all of us at almost anything we were doing. Because he was so willing, I guess we should have been more careful about the things we taught him. He trusted us totally, and if we said it was okay to do something, it was okay with him.

I was away at college when my two younger brothers found another way to be entertained—teaching Butch to harass the garter snakes that lived in the fields. They taught him to grab the snake and toss it end-over-end through the air, then grab it and do it again. This was a real accomplishment, for most often a dog won't even see a snake—it doesn't smell like something he should chase or be interested in, and it's probably best that way.

One afternoon as my brothers Kel and Joel headed up the hill to get the cows in for the evening milking, Butch found a rattlesnake. He didn't know any difference in it and the garter snakes that were so fun to play with, so he grabbed it and tossed it in the air. On the way up it bit him in the loose folds of skin under the jaw. My brothers brought Butch home, terrified that our friend was in mortal danger. There was no anti-venom around in those days, and nothing a vet would do that couldn't be done at home, so Dad lanced the wound to allow it to drain, and told my brothers they would just have to wait and see the consequences of their somewhat irresponsible dog training. As you can guess, they were really heartsick for our friend.

Butch lay nearly motionless in his dog house for most of three days, with dad checking to see that the wound was constantly draining. Then, Butch got up, started walking around and eating, and promptly got well. Needless to say, he didn't play any more snake games. This was probably our family's best lesson in staying far away from things or situations that seemed harmless but could lead to danger.

Chapter 26
Black Canyon

Black Canyon, near Grace, Idaho, is a strange and wonderful place. Looking west from town, all you see is the flat valley floor covered with fields and a few small groups of trees where farmers have homes. A mile or so out of town are two large siphons that take the flow of Bear River from a small dam just above town to a power plant downstream and to the west, hidden on the river bottom. Just past the siphons you see bridge abutments in the middle of the flat, with some small juniper trees scattered about. Then, suddenly, the earth falls away into a canyon a hundred feet or more across and seeming that in depth. The canyon walls are broken lava rock, spectacularly scenic and obviously dangerous to get around on, and in the bottom of the canyon is a small, clear, trout-looking stream, enough to make any fisherman stand on the bridge and look longingly for a trail down.

Bear River used to flow through here, but since the river was put in the power-plant siphons the canyon is left some of the year to mostly spring-fed water, clear and cold.

There is a rudimentary trail to the river, the kind a fisherman likes, for the obvious lack of use means not too many other fishermen go there. However, at the water's edge the trail disappears and the fisherman is left to pick his way along the blocks of jagged rock to find a place to cast a fly. Sometimes it means jumping from rock to rock, sometimes going around those with no easy access, and often the way around is blocked with thick brush or guarded by stinging nettle.

The river is just as treacherous, with holes camouflaged by moss or small, soft piles of sand that will swallow up your boot and the length of a leg if stepped in carelessly. It discourages all but the most avid (or crazy) of the fishermen. The rewards for these intrepid individuals, however, are worth the struggle. The sometimes tiny potholes, filled with clear, cold, deep, dark water hold some remarkable rainbow trout, though they can be challenging to sneak up on and fish for effectively. Further downstream are some large, still, deep pools surrounded by willows, looking like wonderful places to grow trout. The scenery is enhanced by groups of Douglas fir and cottonwood trees that add shade and mystery. Blue Herons, ducks, and many others nest here, all signs of civilization disappear, and you are left to yourself to soak up the remarkable ambience. All in all, the lure of the unknown, the tempting promise of an experience to remember is more than most true fishermen are willing to resist in spite of the hazards.

Black Canyon is a lot like life. There are great, remarkable rewards and exciting experiences for those willing to make the effort to explore the possibilities. "Remember," the sage said, "not even a turtle gets anywhere until it sticks its neck out." Many trips to the depths of this canyon have taught me that gaining something worthwhile always takes some effort, and to get to the really good places, in life or the canyon, may take effort greater than most will put forth, making the experience all the more rewarding for those who will extend themselves to that level.

Black Canyon, 1973

Chapter 27
Black Canyon in Winter

Difficult as it is to travel in summer, this canyon gets next to impossible in winter. The rocks are slippery with snow and ice, some of the water is ice-covered, trails are hidden, and the weather can change instantly from cool to frigid. Nobody should try to even get to the river bottom in winter, let alone travel any distance in the canyon.

There are two accesses to the canyon, the upper one being the bridge west of Grace, and another at the power plant a few miles downstream. Dad had noticed signs of wild mink and muskrats in the canyon when he had been there in summer, and figured that they could be trapped for pelts to supplement our meager winter income, if he could find a way to get them out. Never one to be sensible if there was an adventure involved, he decided that if someone would drop him off with a load of traps at the upper bridge, he could set a trap line all the way down to the lower canyon access, and then he'd not have to backtrack. Mother took a good book to read while she waited, dropped him off, then drove to the lower access parking area to wait for him to appear. There is no doubt in my mind that if she fully understood the condition of the canyon there would have been no way she would be willing to do this, even for her crazy, adventurous husband.

It worked. Dad set traps all the way down the canyon, met Mother where she waited, and they came home, Mother happy he was okay, and Dad smug in his success at beginning to trap in a new, virgin area. A couple of days later, I got to accompany Mother to repeat the trip while he checked the traps for results, but I was too young to go down the canyon with him. The traps did yield some pelts, and the journey was repeated, successfully, again and again before spring.

It was much later, when I was a teenager, that Dad finally told me how he had struggled to keep from being hurt in those hazardous trips. I had noticed it was only that one winter that he had trapped there. I guess the lesson in this is that there is a slight difference in brave and foolish, but it's important to recognize that difference.

Chapter 28
Keith in Black Canyon

One of the outstanding characteristics of Black Canyon is that it seems to always be at least one step ahead of the fishermen who try to conquer it. When it cooperates, the fisherman has a great time, but when the forces align against you, it can be brutal.

One summer day years ago, Dad and my cousin, Keith, decided to see if they could find a short cut to some great fishing holes deep in the heart of the canyon. Dad knew a farmer that lived just above that area, and they parked at his farm and went to see if they could find a trail into the canyon. The farmer was doubtful, but from the upper rim, it looked as if they could make it down, so they started jumping from lava rock to lava rock. The descent was scary, but they were almost to the river when they walked out onto a big rock and realized the next jump was the last one, it would be easy from there. Dad jumped to a smaller rock, then down to the river bottom, and felt success.

Then the canyon decided to get its revenge for being violated by an entry other than on the usual trail. Looking to follow Dad to the river, Keith thought he could make it to a patch of greenery and save one jump, but as he stretched to make the leap, he felt his jeans split in the crotch, all the way around. As he came down into the vegetation, he realized it was stinging nettle. Instead of fishing, Keith spent most of the afternoon sitting in the cold water trying to get relief, knowing the infamous canyon had won again.

Chapter 29
Largest Trout

All the times we fished in Black Canyon, we suspected there were large trout in some of the big pools there, but we never could get one. I remember I caught one that was about three pounds, certainly a respectable size, but not huge by Idaho standards.

I was home from college and my younger brothers said, "Let's go to Black Canyon, we haven't been there lately." It took me probably my usual three seconds or so to be ready, and we headed out. We parked at the upper bridge and hiked down the trail to the river, then fished downstream from there. We had good luck, caught several, though no big ones, then started fishing back up the river toward the truck.

At one of the big, deep holes I fished through the lower end with no results, then hopped out on a large rock that was further out in the pool. I looked down into the deep part of the pool, and at the edge of some moss, suspended in the clear water, was the trout of my dreams, just lazing away the afternoon. I was suddenly frozen in place, knowing how easily trout are scared by movement. The water was still, it was evident that he was not actively feeding, and if I tried to go back the way I had come he would probably be spooked. Casting quietly and carefully, I put my fly past his nose, and he ignored it. I cast again, and he ignored it again. I was really nervous, knowing that he could turn and swim into the moss or dive into the dark water below and be gone for good. Logic said to try another fly pattern, and I did. Still he ignored the fly, it just wasn't feeding time.

When a fisherman is in a situation like this, the best thing is to stay calm, but it is also the hardest to do.

There, little more than a fishing pole length away from me, was a wild rainbow trout of probably five pounds—and I'm to stay calm? Luckily, there were some strands of moss just on my side of his head, and I'm sure that saved me from being spotted. "Quietly change hooks and try again, and again," I counseled myself.

I dropped a hook just on the other side of the fish, finally he cooperated, I set the hook, and suddenly he was ripping line from my reel as he tore down the length of the pool. The power and speed was totally unexpected, but the drag on my fly reel was dependable, and took care of me. No way was I going to let this one get away. The fight lasted several minutes, with both of my brothers cheering me on, excited to see the trout jump into the air again and again, shaking his head at us.

When he came into my net, I finally relaxed, grinned, and knew I had won. Then I could expound to my younger brothers the virtues of patience and perseverance, taking all the credit as if fisherman's luck had nothing to do with it.

My brother, Kel, in Black Canyon, watched by Rufus, 1977

Chapter 30
First Goose

The first goose I ever brought down was when I was a teenager, hunting with my dad and a cousin, Dave Smith, at the Treasureton Reservoir. From the highway we spotted a flock of geese on the lake, and decided they could be ambushed by someone hidden in the willows at the inlet of Battle Creek, if we could get the geese to go that way when they flew up. Dave and I sneaked into the willows and got as near the water as we possibly could without spooking the birds, and Dad drove around the reservoir to get on the other side of them. When he figured we were in position a few yards apart to cover as much area as possible, he started walking up the shore toward the geese, and of course they flew while he was still well out of range, thinking they were safe.

Dave and I heard the honking as they flew up, and hunkered even lower behind the scattered brush, listening in anticipation as the noise got louder and nearer. Pretty soon I could see through the willows the flapping of wings coming our direction. When they got almost overhead, I raised up and shot. A goose started to fall out of the sky, and I just watched breathlessly as it pinwheeled to the ground, landing with a thump twenty or thirty yards from me. I heard Dave's gun going off, and realized I could maybe have gotten more than one if I had kept shooting instead of just watching the first one fall.

It was only a moment and they were gone up the valley. I yelled at Dave, "I got one," and he said, sounding somewhat confused, "I thought I got it." My pride of bagging my first goose vanished like the rest of the flock had, and I was devastated to think that apparently I had missed, and had watched Dave's goose fall.

I walked over to where the bird had fallen, picked it up, and started toward the sound of Dave's voice. At least I could be the retriever for him. Soon he showed up, also carrying a goose. Each of us had seen only one goose fall, but we each had one. My pride returned, knowing that I had indeed got my first goose. I did feel bad momentarily that the bird dog, Butch, had been walking with Dad and had missed out on the retrieve, but Butch forgave me when I let him carry the goose the rest of the way to the truck.

INTERIM PERIOD I

Chapter 31
Seagull 4th of July

The seagull is Utah's state bird, and is protected from any hunting or harassment. I didn't know this when I was younger, more foolish, and tended to be less than gentle and kind to creatures that could provide entertainment.

One 4th of July a friend and I went to the Great Salt Lake to float in the salty water, enjoy a picnic, and just spend a lazy afternoon. We enjoyed the buoyancy of the water, sunburned our bodies, walked up and down the beach, and then sat on the sand to have lunch. It wasn't a very exciting day so far, and looked like we would be ready for it to be over sooner than we had planned, simply because of running out of things to do that were entertaining to us. Besides that, since neither of us was very creative about making a picnic—we had brought some not-too-appetizing plain tuna fish sandwiches for lunch.

We began munching on potato chips and sandwiches, and soon had company, as a flock of seagulls took an immediate interest. Can they smell tuna as they fly past, we wondered, or are they just used to humans sharing their food with them? We tossed out a few chips and they rushed in to pick them up.

Soon we were tearing off chunks of sandwich, which they loved so much it became a real scramble to see who got each morsel. Finally, we had some entertainment.

I'm not sure who got this bright idea, but we had a pocketful of small firecrackers (it was July 4th, remember?) and soon one was wrapped in a remnant of sandwich, the fuse lighted, and tossed out to see what happened. One of the most aggressive birds swooped in, picked it up, and flew quickly away from those who wanted to steal his lunch. It had flown just a few yards when the firecracker exploded. The charge wasn't big enough to really hurt the gull, but there is no measuring how startling it must have been. The gull dodged, then flew really fast in a large circle, climbing higher and higher above us. It was barely a speck in the blue sky when it leveled off and spent the longest time just circling there.

The thought of what we had done to an innocent, hungry bird took away our enthusiasm for any more sport, and soon we picked up our things and left. Why is it that what seems on the spur of the moment to be fun, sometimes can turn out to be the end of fun?

Chapter 32
Uncle Lew's Goose Hunt

When the younger half of mother and dad's family was growing up, Uncle Lew, one of Dad's brothers, lived with us for a while, then had his own place a mile down the road. He loved to hunt, and sometimes we invited him along on our excursions. One winter's day while I was away at college, my younger brothers planned a trip to Mound Valley to hunt geese. The basic premise of the day was to drive along the road on the west side of Bear River, which was up on the hill high enough that most of the river was visible, and if any geese were spotted, a sneak could be planned. The group scanned most of the river, but the geese weren't there. Finally, in order to make sure nothing was missed, they decided to split up and walk to a couple of the areas that couldn't be seen from the road.

Uncle Lew went one direction, and my brothers took the next bend as their assignment. As they climbed a low ridge to get a better view, they saw Uncle Lew in the distance, down on his hands and knees, crawling toward a group of geese. They immediately recognized, from their elevated vantage point, that there was a problem that our intrepid Uncle didn't see. He, not knowing the area well, had walked near the outside edge of a field and was now sneaking up on a farmer's tame geese. True, they were Canada geese, perhaps a little fatter than wild ones, but colored the same.

My brothers realized there was nothing they could do but watch, so that they did. As Uncle Lew got within range, he raised up and the geese began to scatter. Apparently it didn't dawn on him that they didn't fly far, but they did honk like wild geese, and he brought one down with one shot. He calmly walked over, picked up the goose, and headed for the truck.

The brothers almost rolled down the hill laughing, then collected themselves and met him at the truck. They congratulated him on being the only one to get a goose that day, and never did let on what they had watched.

The obvious lesson from this story is that we always need to know where we stand, where our boundaries are, and whose territory we may be near, or even deep within. What appears to be legal may need some extra thought and examination, as to not only is it legal, but is it ethical.

Uncle Lew, October 1968

Chapter 33
Fat Dogs and Good Wives

Have you ever noticed that some pets are way too fat? These pets can be dogs, cats, horses, or even husbands. Maybe you'll object to my categorizing husbands as pets, but bear with me for a few moments.

A few years ago I had the unpleasant experience of major surgery on my heart, including a quadruple bypass and a pacemaker/defibrillator implant. In subsequent visits with the cardiologist my wife insisted on being included in discussions about diet and exercise. She has always fed us healthfully, I thought, but since these visits she has been almost fanatic on reducing my salt consumption, lowering fat intake, and encouraging me to really enjoy an abundance of vegetables and fruits but still allowing a reasonable intake of dark chocolate. I feel so much better when I follow her eating advice, and am so grateful for the importance she places on the care and feeding of her husband. Now, back to the pets.

Whenever I see a dog that is obviously obese, I wonder why the ones who take care of that pet can't do a better job of it. Obviously, not every pet gets to run free through the pastures like my bird dogs always have, but exercise is only part of the formula for a healthful body. There is an abundance of foods today that are balanced to provide nutrition for virtually any level of activity, speaking both of pet food and human food. We need to be more cognizant of the needs of a diet, rather than the wants.

Chapter 34
Fairview Deer

One of the few years I hunted deer when living in Utah I went with some friends to the mountains outside Fairview, Utah. There are high-elevation roads that travel along the tops of the mountain, where there are broad, open, gentle slopes, but the slopes on either side drop precipitously steep for long distances. We decided to park on top and hunt down, working our way along the gentler ridges until we found where the deer were living.

We did find the deer, and each of us got one. Now the work began, because it was uphill all the way to the truck. After field-dressing the deer, we discussed how the best way would be to get those carcasses to the truck. The consensus was that there were no options—we had to carry them up the hill. Luckily none of the deer were very big, and we were young, so we began. We would load up, struggle up the hill for maybe fifty yards, then stop and rest. It seemed like it would take a long time, but it was early in the day, and our spirits were buoyed by the success of the hunt, and besides, we couldn't have come too far down the slope, could we?

Seemed like lunch time came quickly, and we were still packing deer up the hill. Soon it was mid-afternoon, and we were still slaving away. Now, it was near sundown, and still we had not reached the truck, but could see that we were nearing the road, and that made us feel better.

As we broke out of the trees onto an open ridge we could see the strip of trees where the road was, but it was at the top of a steep incline. On the left, however, there was a nearly level trail that went across a wide, steep basin, and on the other side the road was not so far above the trail. It was tempting, after all the climbing we had done, to take the trail, even though it was obviously longer, because it would be pretty much a level walk.

We were so tired, the thought of one more stretch of steep uphill was too much for some of us. The other three suggested that they would really like to take the trail, hoping I would volunteer to go the steep route and bring the truck. I thought it over and decided that the shorter, but steeper, slope couldn't be much worse, so agreed.

I again hoisted my deer onto my shoulders and started climbing, this time pumped up by the thought that I was almost there, and that I had to get there before the other guys crossed the bowl on the trail. It was a brutal climb, but I made it in good time, threw the deer into the truck, and breathed a sigh of relief.

When I drove to the next ridge, I was quite startled to see how far it was. It hadn't looked very far in the clear mountain air, but I drove and drove, it seemed like, to get to where we were to meet. When I arrived, I parked and walked out on the ridge to see where the guys were. In the failing light I could see them laboring along the trail, still only about halfway across, and stopping often to rest. I felt rested now, and so I went out to meet them and give them some help, as it was almost dark. Again, it was amazing how far it was, and I learned a lesson about life.

As we finally got to the truck, it became very evident that sometimes we have to face up to the steep, difficult grades in life and tackle them head-on, because in the long run that is the simplest way—much more desirable than taking the circuitous route that appears to be easier.

Chapter 35
The Pfeifferhorn

I was living in Salt Lake City in the early 1960s, newly married, a student at the University of Utah, and working part-time. My wife worked full time downtown, and one summer morning I dropped her off at work just before eight a.m., then decided on the spur of the moment to drive up Little Cottonwood Canyon.

It was a beautiful mid-summer day, and the mountains were really inviting. I had not explored that canyon at all, and was enjoying seeing the area when I saw a sign that said, "White Pine Lake Trail." With a name like that, and a little-used path winding up the side canyon through the trees, I knew I would have to get better acquainted with that spot. "No time like the present," I rationalized. It was not even nine in the morning, I didn't have to pick up my wife until five, so I had the day to explore. I parked the car and started up the trail, though I hadn't brought water, lunch or even a day pack.

The trees there are magnificent, pine and fir interspersed with groves of aspen and open meadows, and all in the shelter of high mountain peaks and ridges. It didn't take long to get to White Pine Lake, and as I admired its beauty my eye kept wandering upward to the surrounding mountains. I am part of a family that is seriously afflicted with the disease of "If there is a hill, it's worth climbing," and "That one was good, but now there's another one." There was no conscious decision to go on, I just went.

As I climbed higher, the trail came out into open meadows and ridges with fewer trees. Two large mule deer bucks trotted away as I crested a ridge, and the adrenaline from seeing them gave me new energy. It wasn't long before I was seeing currants ripening on bushes, and realized not only was I hungry, but I hadn't brought anything to eat.

The currants tasted good, and gave up some sugary energy to keep me going.

I knew I was getting a long ways from the car, but also had done enough traveling in this kind of country to know that going down was much faster than the climbing, so I had no worry about getting back on time. Because of my experience in these mountains and others like them, I also knew that I had gained a lot of elevation. Looking across the canyon at other ridge tops told me I was probably within a relatively short distance from a ridge that would have a terrific view, and I went on.

Now the trail had disappeared, and the open ridge was my chosen route. This suited me fine, for the views were extraordinary. About this time, however, came a problem. I became very nauseous, dizzy, and needed to sit down, and right now. I sat on the ground to catch my breath, but it didn't seem to help. Finally I leaned over a rock and threw up, hard, until I was really empty, though that didn't take long, with just some mountain currants and creek water to deal with. I'd never had altitude sickness before, but in a matter of minutes I felt much better, and again my wandering eye got the best of any common sense I may have had, and I took a few steps up the ridge. Hmmm, didn't feel too bad—I'll go a little farther.

Suddenly I crested a ridge and there in front of me was the north end of Utah Valley, a marvelous view, overlooked by Mt. Timpanogus, the peaks of which were much lower from this vantage point than I was used to seeing. To my right, the ridge climbed steeply upward through scattered rocks with grass and wildflowers in between, and I thought, "I'll bet the view is really great from up there," and started climbing again.

As I rounded a rock on the ridge top, all at once it was down every direction, and just in front of me was a rock cairn with a mail box labeled "The Pfeifferhorn, Elevation 11,326".

I opened the box and there was a register of those parties who had succeeded in climbing to this lofty point. Of course, I added my name to the not very long list, and looked at my watch. I had about one-third of the day left, then I was due to be a taxi driver for my working wife in downtown Salt Lake.

Luckily, I had not totally disregarded my physical conditioning, and my legs were strong enough to carry me down the mountain, past the lake and through the towering trees to the car. I drove down the canyon and arrived just a moment before my passenger walked out the door to go home.

I'd like to do that hike again sometime, but with proper preparation, including nutrition, conditioning against altitude sickness, and someone to go with me, both for the enjoyment of sharing the experience and for the safety of not being out somewhere totally unknown to anyone.

Rock cairn with box on top of the Pfeifferhorn, September 1964

Chapter 36
The Non-Bird Dog

While I was working really hard at climbing the corporate ladder some years back, I felt I had no time to do any of the fun things that life with a bird dog entails. My family, however, wanted a dog, because I seemed to be always telling them of past good times with my bird dogs, and one day our daughter Carolyn saw a cute, fluffy, small, curly-haired, really black dog and fell in love. I came home from work and was greeted with enthusiasm from three happy faces: Carolyn; her little brother, Chris; and the dog itself. My wife, however, was afraid I would not approve of a dog that didn't have the bird dog instincts I so love, and was fearful of how I would react. When I saw how the kids felt, what could I do but make room in the yard and in my life for "Cinders".

Chris and Cinders, July 1971

Life in Southern California, where we were at the time, seems to be made bearable for youngsters by a few special things, one being water. Cinders loved to play in the yard with the kids when the hose was on and they all loved it. I would get home from work and be regaled with stories of how Cinders entertained them day after day. I think my prejudices about what kinds of dogs were useful, or at least of some purpose, began to crumble.

Cinders was a great pal for the kids. Playtime seemed endless from morning to night, and even the small barking noises that can be irritating to a bird dog lover didn't bother me that much, as I knew there was an extra playmate loved by the kids.

Chapter 37
Ask, Listen

Some of the most useful lessons come from unexpected sources. Judy and I had just moved to Montpelier, Idaho and were renting an older house while deciding what we wanted to buy. The local railroad switching activities had just been discontinued in the town, and many people were out of work. The whole area seemed down on itself, the mood was one of doom and gloom, and consequently real estate prices were way down, also. I had just left a good-paying position as national sales manager for Pace-Arrow Motor Homes and had some money to use for purchasing a house. We felt the house we were in would be adequate for us, so I went to the real estate office that was handling the rental to see if it was for sale.

I introduced myself to the broker/owner and asked if the house we were renting was for sale, and indeed it was. I asked the price, it was reasonable, and I was ready to make an offer, but the broker went into a ten-minute speech on who could apply and how to qualify for low-income, low-interest loans from Farmers Home Administration. I hadn't asked about loans, as I wanted to make a cash offer, but the broker's assumption, apparently, was that nobody had any money and everyone needed a low-income type loan. I asked something else about the house, he answered it quickly, then went into another lengthy speech on low-interest, low-income loans. I appreciated his knowledge of the topic, but it didn't apply to me. When he wound down, I thanked him for the visit, and left, shaking my head as to his sales technique.

That evening there was a knock on our front door, and when I opened it I found it was the secretary from the real estate office. She looked quickly up and down the street as if to see if anyone had seen her, and asked to come in.

We let her in, and she said, "I hope you won't tell my boss I'm here, but my parents have a house for sale, would you like to see it?" To make the story shorter, we did look at the house the next morning, we liked it even better than the one we were in, made an offer, and paid cash for the house.

There are more lessons from this event, but one of the most important is to ask what the other person wants, then listen for an answer. If the broker had just asked, "Mr. Smith, what would you like to do?" and then listened to my reply, he would have sold us a house.

The house we bought, 1973

Chapter 38
Opportunity

Sometime after the unsuccessful attempt to buy a house from what was apparently the only active real estate office in the town, Judy and I had the idea that perhaps, since we had not yet decided what to do for a living, we should investigate that business. Maybe there was a need for someone who had experience in selling. The state required two years' experience as a sales associate before qualifying for a broker's license to run an office. I didn't feel very good about being affiliated with the "low-interest loans" broker, so we looked in the yellow pages and found a listing for another real estate office. I dialed the number and got no answer. Later I tried again, still no answer. "How do you do business in this town?" I thought.

The next day I called again, and this time the phone was picked up and a tentative voice said, "Hello?" "Not very businesslike," I thought, but asked if this was the real estate office, and the voice said it was. I asked why I didn't get an answer the day before, and he said he had been out of town. "Hmm, no office help," I thought, and made an appointment to meet him.

When I arrived at the address he had given me it was the office of a local attorney, and there was a small real estate sign in the window. The attorney explained that he didn't do much real estate work, but wanted to have the name and license when something came up that was beneficial. After some discussion, I felt we could probably work together, and proposed that I get my real estate license and come run that office for him. He jumped at the chance. I called the Real Estate Commission in Boise, had them mail me the real estate law book, read it, took and passed the exam, and I became a real estate licensee.

All it took to get started was an announcement in the local newspaper that a new office was open, and business started to come in. We operated quite successfully for more than a year, even hiring another licensee from a neighboring town to expand our business area. I wasn't making a lot **of** money, but it was a living, and the pace was satisfying. I got a chance to list a nice-sized ranch property, and it sold quite quickly. I was anticipating a healthy commission, and scheduled a closing. The attorney had been in on a couple of discussions in this sale, but had not really been a factor in any decision making, so I was really surprised when he asked to sit in on the closing. He was my broker, even though I worked pretty much on my own, so of course I agreed.

After the closing, I sat down with the broker to get my commission check, and he began a somber discussion about how he felt he had contributed to the sale, then handed me a check for a small portion of what our agreed-on split in all our other sales had been. I protested, but he insisted he had earned what he was taking, and that was how it was going to be.

I realized that I needed to be in control of my own life, and since the required two-year period of apprenticeship was almost up, I applied for my broker's license. By the time the two-year date rolled around, I was licensed and opened my own office, happily in competition with the two offices that had furnished an eye-opening introduction to real estate in Idaho.

Chapter 39
Sam

Montpelier, Idaho had been our home for a couple of years. The home we had purchased (see "Ask, Listen") was nearly modernized and comfortable for us, and had a big lot with a garden spot. The back yard was only partially fenced, and we didn't bother to do any more to make it private as the neighbors were not really close to us, so sometimes we would find neighborhood animals crossing through or playing on the lawn. It wasn't a stressful thing to us, in fact, sometimes we quite enjoyed their antics.

One day we noticed a female bird dog, spotted like a German Shorthair pointer, but white with black spots, not the usual brown. We decided she must be crossed with something else, but it didn't matter to us, because she wasn't our dog (or so we thought at the time). Our standard practice was to be careful not to feed or otherwise encourage any of these strays to stay around, but this one stayed anyway. After a couple of days, we began to worry if she had eaten, and sure enough, we fed her. That did it, she promptly adopted us, and we began calling her Sam, but still let her run loose in the yard just in case she wanted to return to wherever she came from.

Not long after this, we found that apparently the strays eat well enough, as one morning Sam brought home part of what she had been eating in the night. This disturbed us a little, as the "snack" was the lower twenty inches or so of a horse's leg, including a hoof with a shoe attached. We never did learn whose horse it had been, where it came from, or if the horse had been dead when Sam found it.

Sam stayed with us a matter of months, and it became evident that she was pregnant.

It didn't take more than a conversation with the neighbor just behind us to determine who the father was, as the neighbor had seen his red-bone hound and Sam together.

When the puppies came, they were adorable, as most puppies are, and we decided early which one we would keep, and succeeded in giving away the others. The one we chose to keep was more typically bird-dog than most, which suited me, and we named him Rufus. It was only a matter of weeks when he was weaned and on his own, and had really become part of the family, when Sam disappeared. We still don't know if she had just decided to go to her previous home again, or if, as we like to think, she somehow knew we needed a bird dog, showed up, worked her way firmly into our hearts, produced a puppy for us to raise, then, her mission accomplished, chose to go on with her life. We thank her for Rufus.

Sam and a playmate, 1974

THE "RUFUS" ERA

Chapter 40
Bird Dog in Training

There were several phases to Rufus' training. The most important to us was that he became a family dog, and this Rufus excelled at. He loved us and the girls, and became a part of our family as a puppy. This is one of the reasons we enjoyed training him to be a bird dog by himself, rather than having a companion to train at the same time. Some think that a dog needs other canine companionship, but we always felt we did better with his full attention on the trainer and the training.

As this initial bonding and indoctrination into family routines was accomplished, he began to grow bird dog skills, such as retrieving. It is natural for a puppy to want to chew things, and hold things in its mouth, carrying them around as if he owned them. This develops into the retrieving function, and the only real chore for the trainer is to get him to learn to release on command, and realize that the trainer is in charge of when to retrieve and when to release. It is such a pleasure to see a new dog learn that his trainer will extend much appreciation at the end of a successful retrieve. Repetition is a big thing, and letting kids throw things to be retrieved is good training for both, if the kids realize they need to enforce the completion of the retrieve.

Obedience training is interwoven into all of the training of a dog. From the very beginning it must learn to obey "no" and how to listen for the owner's instruction on everything it is told to do. How this is done is through consistency, by never letting up or giving mixed signals. Whether training dogs or children, the most important thing is to never give a command that you don't expect to be obeyed, and make sure each command is enforced until it is completed.

Rufus was less than a year old when hunting season came, but we felt he was ready to go hunting and try his retrieving skills. He had learned well how to fetch a stick thrown, whether in the field or in the river, and would faithfully follow rather than go off on his own. It was important to us that he be given the right training without any outside interference, so I arranged with a landowner friend in the Geneva valley to hunt ducks on the canal in his fields. To get there, we went down Wood Canyon, and in one of the ponds in the canyon there were a couple of ducks, sitting near enough to the dam that we could sneak up on them and get a shot. Perfect, I thought.

We went down the road far enough to be out of sight, then came up the outflow stream to the dam. Keeping Rufus behind me, I crept up over the dam, and as the ducks flew up I downed one of them, figuring that was enough for Rufus' first lesson. I told him, "Fetch, Rufus, go get it!"

He saw the duck fall, ran to water's edge, swam out to where the crippled duck was paddling around, but the duck dove under the water. Rufus, confused at this new development, swam in a circle, looking for the duck. Suddenly it surfaced, and Rufus again swam toward it, again it dove, and this time it came up right under the dog. This was really confusing to Rufus, who didn't know what to do, but tried to grab the duck, and it dove again. By now, Rufus had had enough of this and swam to the edge of the water and stood and watched as the duck surfaced once again, this time nearer the other edge of the pond. I decided it was time for some assistance, so I shot the duck again, and it died instantly. "Now," I thought, "Rufus can fetch it!" But he had lost interest. He didn't want any more to do with that evasive creature, even when it just lay there.

The pond wasn't very deep, and by this time the duck had drifted near enough to the edge that I could get to it, so I waded out, got the duck, came back to the bank and held it up for Rufus. "Here," I said, "fetch," and tossed the duck up the bank a few feet for Rufus to fetch. He eagerly ran to the duck, picked it up, and took it out into the pond where he had first seen the duck and left it there, and swam back. I guess he thought that was where it belonged. I waded out again, got the duck, and carried it to the truck, showing Rufus that to retrieve means to bring to our possession, hoping he got the message.

We continued on to the canal in the fields, all the time trying to figure out what Rufus needed to learn, and how to teach it. Somehow it soaked in as we traveled, for when I downed a duck in the first group we jumped, Rufus ran to it and retrieved it like an old pro. Then we found a big group of ducks and downed more than one, and Rufus brought one, then another, and I decided he was trained.

From that day on, he was a super retriever, never giving up until he had completed his job.

Chapter 41
Rufus, a Good Dad

Not long after we got Rufus trained, we got him a playmate, an English Pointer named Rachel. They loved to hunt ground squirrels together, running through the sage brush a few yards apart and surprising the squirrels as they ran from one to the other. They seemed a perfect match, and became very adept at catching squirrels.

Rufus and Rachel had a dozen or so pups one spring. They were so cute, with floppy ears that got in the way of oversize feet as they played, scuffling back and forth, no one dominating but all enjoying the company of each other. It seemed they were always running in an undulating, shifting group of perpetual motion, appearing to be always on the edge of some new disaster. We lived in Maple Canyon outside Bennington, Idaho, at the time, and as summer came, the mornings were apparently made for our enjoyment. As the sun streamed through the maple trees, the grass seemed greener, the sky bluer, the air clearer, and spirits brighter each day than the day before. We had a table and benches on the back lawn to sit and enjoy the warmth of the sun and a morning snack, and visit about the coming day.

Rufus and some of the family, 1976

One beautiful morning, as Judy went out the back door toward the table, hands carrying a tray of breakfast goodies, mind deep in thought, she looked up and saw the whole group of pups headed across the lawn to greet her, ears flopping, bumping into each other as they ran, all seemingly grinning ear to ear, so happy to see their human, and bent on greeting her in the fashion they thought best, by totally surrounding her feet.

She hardly had time to realize what peril there was to her continued movement, and say, "Oh, no," when Rufus, ever the watchful protector, ran out to the approaching horde, placing himself at the front quarter of the pack, and changed their course to move them across the lawn and harmlessly past the endangered human. By the time they returned, Judy was safely at the table and ready for their enthusiastic greeting. Rufus accepted as his reward a pat on the head and a morsel of something to eat, and knew he had done his job well.

Chapter 42
Brother-in-law's Goose

My oldest sister, Mignon, was married to Dave Jensen for over sixty years before they both passed away, just months apart. They were a devoted couple, each willing to do most anything to make the other happy. Dave wasn't a fanatic hunter like some of the family seems to be, but was willing to go along when we wanted company because he thought Mignon would want him to. One fall my brother Kel came for a goose hunt, and we invited Dave to go with us out to the Geneva Valley where the geese liked to stay.

We parked the truck just at daylight and started across the fields toward the river. The whole area was covered with a ten or twelve foot deep blanket of dense ground fog, with an occasional break of a few feet. Since we knew the area well, there was no problem moving toward where we wanted to be, and we separated a few yards as we walked.

Dave was probably fifty or sixty feet behind me as we were crossing a meadow. I heard a goose honk directly ahead, looked up, and through a tiny break in the fog saw just a glimpse of a body sailing toward Dave. I yelled, "Here he comes, Dave," thinking Dave would enjoy the view as I had, seeing a momentary flash of wings, and then it would be gone in the fog. Instead, a moment after I had yelled, his gun went off. "That's interesting," I thought, maybe there was a bigger break in the fog. Then, "thunk" echoed across the field, and I realized he had got the goose. He later described it as, "When you yelled, I just pointed my gun up, the goose appeared in the right spot, so I pulled the trigger. It fell."

Funny how a good bird dog seems to know where to go even when visibility is so limited as to virtually blind us humans, but Rufus' retrieve was perfect, and the day was off to a great beginning.

Chapter 43
Bigfoot Lives at Bloomington Lake

One of our family's favorite Southern Idaho destinations on a hot summer day is Bloomington Lake, situated at about 8,000 feet in the mountains west of Bear Lake. This is a glacial lake, a beautiful cirque, with precipitous slopes on one side that keep snow most of the summer, and across the lake an easier, but still very steep, south-facing slope. A visit in the earlier part of the summer will often require hiking to be on the south-facing slopes, as the other side will be still too snowy to travel.

It was on one of these June or early July days that my embryonic belief in Bigfoot matured. I think I had always hoped that there was a creature like that, and if so, I thought it would be really great to see one, or at least some sign of one. On the other hand, maybe the lack of scientific proof of their existence is what makes the tales about them so intriguing. As I was growing up, anytime I was in really remote, rugged country, I could daydream one or more of them into existence. I had concluded that they have a highly developed sixth sense, one that works better than radar, that can sense human presence early enough and accurately enough to let them move to hidden places before they are spotted, so never actually seeing the creature doesn't mean they don't exist.

On the slopes above Bloomington Lake the early summer wildflowers grow profusely. My camera was the impetus to climb and explore new views and angles to photograph these and the spectacular cliffs that top the almost impossibly steep slope.

The view of the deep lake became more spectacular, bluer and darker, the higher I climbed, and as I got within a couple hundred feet of the base of the cliffs at the top of the slope above me I could see that the cliffs are very irregular, filled with tunnels and caves that let the sky above show through and some that have dark interiors that could hold almost anything. I was intent on taking photos of the flowers, the majesty of the rocks against the sky, the few trees that perch precariously on the top, and the lake below when suddenly I heard a crashing above me, coming from the cliffs.

I looked up and saw some really large chunks of snow, a couple of feet or more in diameter, coming down the slope, just off to the side of where I was standing. There was no reason for that snow to break away in the nice, calm afternoon, especially since all the exposed snow had long since melted. My inside got a really strange feeling, and I lost all desire to be there taking pictures or doing anything else but leaving, so that is what I did, as expeditiously as I could on the steep slope. I calmed down again as soon as I was back on the trail around the lake, headed toward the truck.

Thinking back on this incident has brought the following conclusions: (1) If there is a Bigfoot, and that's what started the snow rolling, he has no desire to hurt me, just to warn me that I'm traveling where he doesn't want me, as the snow chunks were off to the side of where they would be dangerous. (2) Any human presence high on the north rim of that cirque is so infrequent that it would be a perfect place for an early-summer nursery. (3) Those plants that grow from corms or other potential food sources are plentiful there in the early summer. (4) The elevation and open meadows of wild flowers give a perfect view of anyone approaching. (5) There is no reason in Bigfoot's mind for anyone to see him other than idle curiosity, and he will not put up with that!

Bloomington Lake, 1995

Chapter 44
Tulip Crossed Up

A tulip is a flower, we all know that, but Tulip was also the name of a horse we owned some years ago. I don't remember where she got her name, but I remember her and where she came from — a sheep rancher in the Geneva Valley (Bear Lake County, Idaho) raised her on his ranch and offered her to us as a three-year old, untrained, hardly even halter broke. She seemed to have a good, even disposition and was reasonably well put together, so we bought her at a low price. Judy asked why I would buy an unbroke horse; I had never broke one before, and I simply replied, "She's never been broke, so she won't know the difference." Thus started the training of Tulip to become a riding horse.

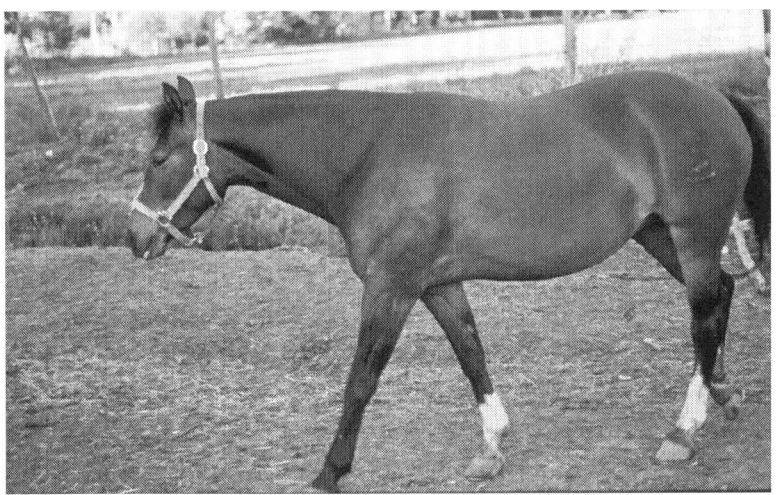

Tulip, 1975

Since she had a mellow disposition, all went pretty well at first, but as is the case with many novice horse trainers, I was more interested in results than in the process, and any good, experienced horse trainer will tell you that is backwards.

The process, though tedious to an impatient personality, is what makes a good riding horse. The first flaw in my method showed up when one day I had Judy saddle the trained horse we had so we could pony Tulip with a saddle on, then with me in the saddle. The dry run with the saddle went good, and I got (again as inexperienced trainers will) impatient at getting aboard, so I told Judy to shorten up the lead rope and I'd try her out. Since Judy's experience matched mine, she agreed, and I climbed on. We walked around the small pasture evenly, and again inexperience got ahead of good sense. I urged the group to a trot, and when the saddle began to bounce, so did Tulip — quite vigorously. It wasn't really hard bucking, but it felt like it to me, and I remember coming out of the saddle, seeing Tulip disappear from beneath me, and thinking, "Now, do I want to land on that rock or can I miss it?" The ground was hard, and so was my fall, but I wasn't injured, so training continued.

Several days later we tried again, all went well, and it was only a few days more until Tulip and I were navigating the sagebrush hills together and both enjoying the trips. One morning as we rode I got off to open a gate, led Tulip through, let Judy ride through on her horse, and closed the gate.

I put the reins back over Tulip's head, got back on, and started up the trail when she just came apart. Pulling on the reins got no response, yelling made her go faster, and almost instantly we were galloping full speed along a narrow, winding trail through the sagebrush. I had no idea why she seemed to have forgotten everything I had taught about control, but after a hundred yards or so she just stopped and looked confused. I quickly got off, and she settled down.

I petted her, talked to her, and realized as I moved around her that when I had put the reins over her head after the gate was closed I had crossed the reins under her jaw, so when I moved the reins for a left turn, she was being told to turn both directions. No wonder she was confused. I fixed the problem, remounted, and from then on she was a good horse. Have you known humans that had that kind of misapplied training? I have.

Chapter 45
Persistence Delivers

Rufus loved the hunt, and anything associated with it. I couldn't even target practice without him wanting to retrieve whatever it was I was shooting at. One evening in Maple Canyon I decided to shoot some clay pigeons and went out behind the house with Judy holding Rufus tightly to keep him in check while I sent some targets flying and did my practice. It wasn't long, however, before she relaxed her grip and Rufus took off, bound to retrieve. That was all for the shooting, as he didn't care where he ran.

He scoured the hillside, looking in every sage bush, sniffing every rock, and as time passed I called him, but he wouldn't come back, because he hadn't found anything that he could fetch. We sat down, knowing it may be a while, and waited.

Maple Canyon home, 1975

Rufus kept looking, sniffing, being more persistent than I could believe, when all at once he dove in a sage bush and out flew two Hungarian partridge. I was dumfounded that they would stay there with all the shooting I had done, but they had stayed put until Rufus found them. Then I realized why he had been so persistent—he had been able to smell them, and was determined to flush them out or retrieve them, which ever applied. As soon as they flew, Rufus turned and came to me, as if to say, "Well, you missed again, dummy!" I confessed that I had, and thanked him for being so devoted to getting his job done.

Chapter 46
Look Before You Leap

Rufus loved to go to the real estate office in Montpelier, Idaho with us. I was the broker, Judy tended the front desk, and Rufus mostly lay by my desk, greeting with enthusiasm any visitor.

Patience was not one of his strong points, however, since he was a "person" of action, not one to lay around once he was caught up on the required naps. When he thought it was time to go do something else, he let us know with no uncertainty that he had spent enough time in the office, and began to stand at the glass door in front looking alternately at the out-of-doors and back to us, quietly giving loud and clear the message that it was time to leave that place.

When I finally got my duties to the point that I could go, I would find an excuse to put him in the truck and inspect a property, or perhaps just drive around looking for a property to inspect, Rufus happily moving from side to side in the back of the truck, ears flapping, lips catching the wind and making me wonder if he would blow up like a balloon and float off into space.

One day when I had too much to do to leave the office right away he got more and more disappointed, and finally just lay down by the front window, his nose seeming to get longer and longer with dismay. Finally I completed what was needed and started for the door. He scrambled to attention, tail wagging so hard it seemed to start at his shoulders, and waited for me to open the door.

The truck was parked two or three parking spaces up the street from the office, and as I opened the door Rufus charged out, dashed across the sidewalk, made a mighty leap into the air to get in the back of the truck, he thought, and landed full speed on the top of the trunk of a car that was parked out front.

As soon as he landed, he realized it was not the right place, and, wow, did he look embarrassed. He carefully and sheepishly jumped down to the sidewalk and trotted nonchalantly up the street to the truck, where he waited in a subdued manner for the tailgate to be opened. As soon as I opened it he jumped in, and suddenly everything was okay again. Interesting how quickly he could forgive (and forget) his silly, earlier mistake and move on to what lay ahead.

The office, 1977

Chapter 47
Sandhill Crane Goose

One of the most gratifying shots I ever made on a goose was while hunting on the Bear River, near Geneva, Idaho. Judy had come along for the fun of watching the action, and there was a lot of it—a multitude of sandhill cranes were in the valley congregating for the migration south, the noise of their cackling sometimes becoming almost deafening as they circled overhead, landed nearby, and encouraged each other to get ready to go.

We were hiding in a depression formed by a former bend of the river, behind some brush that gave pretty good cover, and had managed to get a goose from some flocks that flew by in between the groups of cranes. It was a beautiful evening, and we were pretty relaxed, not taking the hunt too seriously. I had propped my gun against the brush and we were just visiting, enjoying the huge numbers of cranes as they wheeled by.

I heard a crane cackling behind me, and looked over my shoulder as a classic v-formation of cranes, four on one side and five on the other, approached, very low to the ground. I said to Judy, "Wow, those are in real shotgun range, too bad they're cranes, not geese." We watched them as they flew by almost directly overhead. We could hear the sound of their wings in the air, and just as they flew over us, one of them honked like a goose. "That is a goose," I said, realizing the third one back on the left leg of the "v" was not a crane at all, but a goose trying to sneak past us. I whirled, grabbed my gun, did a snap shot and the goose tumbled out of formation to the ground. The cranes never broke formation, just continued on toward the river. Rufus retrieved the goose, and I was a hero in my wife's eyes, which is all I really wanted, anyway.

Chapter 48
Joe the Horse

Joe was beautiful. He was of classic cow-horse build, not too tall, heavily muscled, strong legs, good feet, an intelligent eye, and bay (my favorite horse color). Judy and I owned him when we lived in Liberty, Idaho, in the Bear Lake Valley. This is wonderful riding country, surrounded by national forest with endless trails, trees, streams, and views. Joe walked nicely, covered a lot of miles in a day, and carried me without any discomfort to either of us.

That is, until one day when we were riding with the Bear Lake Rangers riding group through the hills near North Canyon. The trail was reasonably clear, but we came to some down timber, a couple of fallen logs. The first was an easy step over, but the second required a little jump to get across. When Joe hopped the log, apparently he thought it was fun, for he just kept jumping, then it turned to bucking, and we bounced off the trail through the trees. He wouldn't listen to my directions, verbal or by the reins, but just kept hopping. I decided that to stay on him in the timber was more dangerous than I wanted, so picked a reasonable clearing and bailed off. He took a few more jumps, then stopped and looked around as if to say, "Why did you get off, that was fun!" I led him back to the trail, got on, and continued the ride, quite uneventfully.

I decided Joe was okay, and we rode several more nice rides. Then one day we were riding up a road through a neighbor's hay field, when with no warning or indication, Joe started bucking, turned off the road into the field, and got really serious with the bucking program, until he landed in a hole, lost his balance and went down. As he fell I kicked out of the stirrups and fell to the side, not wanting to be under him if he went all the way to the ground. And down he did go, landing on his side and rolling over.

When he rolled, the saddle horn caught the hay in a windrow and as he stood up, a section of windrow several feet long came up with him. He apparently didn't like the apparition that took my place in the saddle, bucked until it fell off, went a few steps and stopped to see if I had arranged that. I promptly took the credit, hoping it would help him learn that bucking was not an approved activity. I mounted up and rode home with no more trouble, but thought there would need to be some remedial riding.

Joe, the horse, 1995

A few days later one of the neighbors was gathering cattle from the forest, a hard day's riding, and consented to take Joe along for the experience. His boys were real cowboys, good riders, and I thought that kind of riding was just what Joe needed. One of his boys, Brian Parker, rode Joe, then let his girlfriend ride Joe, and all day the trip was good.

The cows were in the corral, everyone was tired, and just a few animals to be sorted out then the day was over. As Brian started to cut a cow out of the herd, suddenly Joe came apart again, and for no apparent reason bucked high in the air. Brian came down hard on the saddle horn and decided Joe was not a pleasant ride after all.

That was all for Joe. I sold him by the pound, not daring trust his riding to anyone. We need to be as good on the inside as we look on the outside, so those who need to trust us can truly depend on us.

Chapter 49
Rufus' Baby Duck

I was fishing in Black Canyon west of Grace, Idaho and Rufus, my best friend and most faithful companion, came along for the trip. He was always busy, sniffing with his bird dog nose the exotic smells of a new area and exploring around the lava rocks and all along the river bottom.

A really avid fly fisherman will not generally put up with the unintentional disturbance to fly fishing that a roaming dog creates, but who could turn down Rufus' intense look that said, even if unspoken, "Why can't I go along, you know how I enjoy going?" I guess my enjoyment matched his, even if the fishing was not always all I wanted it to be. The journey with my friend was the pleasure.

An angler in Black Canyon, 1973

We had fished quite a distance up the canyon and Rufus had settled into a routine of circles out a few hundred feet to new places and then back to check on my progress, and to hope that sometime I would let him fetch the fish that was on my line, knowing that I wouldn't, but still seeming to hope for this activity. The instinct to help by fetching is almost insatiable, and not at all hidden, in a good bird dog.

I had just reeled in my fly line to move to a new spot, when I looked up and here came Rufus around a big rock, trotting proudly with a mouth full of something. As he got near, I could see that it was a half-grown duck he had caught, and being the soft-mouthed retriever he was, he had not injured it, but the duck was holding its head up and tolerating, if not enjoying, the ride. Rufus eagerly came to me with his prize, showing me that he, too, could catch something.

Now, I thought, this is a real dilemma. Rufus is a good bird dog, one that will always retrieve what we're hunting, and I don't want to change or damage that instinct by telling him to not do the retrieve he is doing. On the other hand, he can't just go off on his own and bring in a duck whenever he wants. I decided that maybe a conversation would be in order, and I said, "Rufus, that's a good retrieve, but you know that it isn't duck season, you should let the duck go."

He looked at me for just a moment, then put his head down and opened his mouth. The little duck plopped out on the sand, stood up, looked around, shook its feathers into place and then calmly walked off into some nearby cattails. Rufus seemed completely happy with this as I patted him and thanked him for understanding. I honestly don't remember how the fishing was that day, but I remember Rufus and his comprehension of more English than I expected. Life can be like that, with lessons in good behavior to emulate coming at really unexpected times.

Chapter 50
The Beginning of an Era

Judy and I had determined we were going to move to Three Rivers, California, from Idaho, mostly to be near some of her family members as they grew older, but also because we loved living in that beautiful, comfortable area. The South Fork of the Kaweah River, especially, where Judy's grandfather had purchased a section of land in 1908, holds a magic that still settles our souls.

We arranged for Randy Stoor to take over our Montpelier office, to continue the real estate and construction activities there, and we brought our travel trailer and parked it at Judy's mother's place on the South Fork. I planned to commute enough to keep my hand in the Idaho business as long as needed. We owned some property in Three Rivers, but vacant lots only, so began looking for a place to rent for a while.

Judy talked with an acquaintance, Gladys Lukehart, about finding a rental, but Gladys was very evasive. It wasn't long before she called us and said we needed to talk. We met at her office, and again she was vague about details, but said there were people from Los Angeles that had purchased a property on the South Fork that were looking for someone to live there and manage the ranch since they would only be coming to Three Rivers occasionally. She gave us an address and said she and the new owners would meet us there that Saturday if we were interested. We talked it over and decided to at least meet them.

As we arrived at the address, we found it to be one of the most beautiful places on the South Fork, about 18 acres of mostly gentle slopes, an old barn, a nice house, and bordering the river just above Judy's favorite childhood swimming hole.

The fences and pastures showed some years of minimal maintenance, but the site was wonderful. When Gladys welcomed us to the place, she introduced us to the owner, William (Bill) Shatner, the famous "Star Trek" actor. He was accompanied by his wife, Marcy, and his business manager, Victor Meschures. After a brief tour of the grounds, we went in the house to discuss possible business arrangements.

Victor said one of their goals was to make this a working ranch, and could we raise some cattle or something to make that work? We discussed irrigation, fences, and the rejuvenation of the necessary things to accomplish that, when Victor asked how many cows we could raise on 18 acres. Since none of us had significant knowledge of how much irrigation water was available, I suggested that four or five would probably be a prudent number. Victor looked really disappointed, and said, "I was hoping maybe forty or fifty. How do you raise cows, anyway?" I reviewed briefly the life cycle of raising cattle for market, finishing with "and when the steers get to maybe a thousand pounds, they are ready for slaughter." Victor asked, "Why don't we keep them until they are thousands of pounds?" then paused a moment as I looked at him speechless, and said, "Oh, I guess they don't grow that way, do they?" I knew immediately we had some educating to do at the business office.

While I was justifying how many cows could be raised on that small acreage, Judy interrupted with, "Why don't we raise horses instead of cows, they smell better?" Bill, who had been mostly listening, jumped into the conversation with "Oh, I like horses much better than cows!"

That settled it. The decisions were: (1) Judy and I would manage the ranch, (2) I would start shopping immediately for quarter horses, preferably of cutting horse breeding, and (3) all the other details like irrigation and fences we would work out over time. We happily moved into the house to begin our experience of hobnobbing with (and educating) the rich and famous.

Chapter 51
A Horse Buy Mistake

After we had been in the quarter horse business with William (Bill) Shatner a couple of years, we took some young horses to a sale in Sacramento. While we were there, we wanted to buy a gelding for riding around the ranch, if we could get one that seemed suitable, and at a reasonable price. Usually Judy and I went to the sales, but this time Bill said, "I'd like to go with you and bid on a horse, it looks like it would be fun," so he came along.

At the sale we met up with one of the families that we had become business friends with, Jerry and Nancy Rapp, from Napa. They were pretty new in the business, also, and we got along well. They had a son, Phillip (later a leading cutting horse trainer), who was about twelve years old at the time. He was a good conversationalist, and Bill really enjoyed visiting with him.

In order to be as visible as possible (an asset in building our reputation in the business) we had positioned ourselves on the front row of the sale, right in front of the auctioneer, Duane Pettibone. He also had become a friend, and we were comfortable dealing with him. We had gone through the sale catalog before the sale and marked those geldings we might want to bid on, then previewed each one. We knew pretty much which horses would be acceptable for our ranch horse purposes and how much we would be willing to pay for each of them.

As the sale proceeded, we bid on a few, but the prices went higher than our predetermined limits. Bill was enjoying bidding, and followed our business plan very well. We were the high bidder on a nice gelding at a really good price, but shortly after he announced "Sold!" the auctioneer motioned he needed to see me outside.

He explained that the horse was meant to have a reserve price higher than we had bid, but the owner's agent that was to bid it up had missed his opportunity, and the horse wasn't supposed to be sold at that price. In asking us to give up the purchase, he gave us the option to hold him to the sale if we needed to, but would like to have us not buy the horse. I agreed, told Bill we didn't get the horse, and we went back to bidding on our sale list.

It wasn't long before a really nice gelding, Dandy Doc Tucker, came in the ring, a beautiful five-year old bay with a petite head, big hip, short back, and well trained. We had allowed a budget price of $1,600, and the bidding passed that, so we dropped out. I went out to the preview area to refresh my memory on the next one we had on the list. As I inspected the horse, I half-listened to the auction going on, and heard the auctioneer announce that Dandy sold for $2,600. Not thirty seconds later Bill appeared, looking really frantic, and excitedly said, "I just bought that horse, what do I do?"

Then he told me what had happened. He was visiting with Phillip Rapp, having one of their animated conversations, smiling and nodding at Phillip, when he looked up the auctioneer, still smiling and nodding, and of course the auctioneer took that as a very clear buying signal, slammed down his gavel, pointed at Bill, and said, "Sold!" In reply to his question of what to do, I simply said, "Pay for it!"

Yes, I realized that the auctioneer owed me a favor, and we could have cancelled the sale, but it wouldn't have been good for our business reputation, Bill being as visible as he was. Besides, it was a really good lesson for Bill.

Bill on Dandy, the ranch gelding, 1982

Chapter 52
Rufus and the Coyote Trap

Living in the foothills below Sequoia Park, specifically on the South Fork of the Kaweah River and having horses to ride, has been Judy's dream all her life, since spending most of her summers there as a youngster with her grandparents. I gladly joined in her enthusiasm when we got a chance to move there, on a ranch that had easy access to mountain roads for riding. Our bird dog, Rufus loved it there also, and especially liked the trips up the canyon where he could run alongside the horses and explore and sniff as we rode.

I was often busy with ranch work, and Judy rode without me sometimes. One day she had gone riding alone and a couple of hours later she came galloping down the road yelling for help. "Rufus is caught in a coyote trap," she shouted as she rode up. I asked where, jumped on the ATV, and headed up the hill. As I neared the area where I expected to find Rufus I saw him coming down the side of the road, dragging a trap that had him by the toe. It had to be really painful to wrestle it loose from its anchors and head for home.

Having been around and/or using traps all my life, I thought it was no big deal to take it off. I stopped, petted and sympathized with Rufus, then bent down to open the trap. As I put enough pressure on the springs to release the jaws, the trap twisted slightly, and it must have hurt, for Rufus, with a nasty snarl, snapped and bit at my arm. The trap did release, Rufus was free, but I was dumbfounded that he would turn on me, his best friend and obvious benefactor, and try to hurt me. Hadn't I just saved him from further pain and taken away the cause of his hurt? Rufus was immediately grateful to be out of the trap and was obviously sorry that he snapped at me, so I forgave him, of course.

Since that incident, I have tried to keep in mind that I can't always measure the degree of distress that may be in another's system, whether physical or otherwise, and when they turn on me viciously it may be that the problem isn't with me at all, but is because of unseen things going on inside them. This thought makes it easier, even almost automatic, to forgive and overlook entirely any seemingly offensive words or actions.

Chapter 53
"Humanizing" a Foal

Bill (William Shatner) was pretty familiar with horses, including experience with horses on the sets of some movies, and one of the things he really looked forward to was "humanizing" a foal, that is, getting a new baby to accept a human presence and submit to training right after its birth. When a mare foaled, he wanted to be called right away, so if his schedule permitted, he could come to the ranch and spend time with the baby. He did get to come up and welcome some babies, surrounding them with loving arms and cooing soft words, and it probably was good for them, but we couldn't always tell. Foals of the cow horse breeding we liked were naturally of a gentle disposition anyway.

One especially perky filly seemed to be a favorite of Bill's, even though she was out of an Appaloosa ranch mare, not a quarter horse. On one of his ranch visits he climbed over the wooden fence into the pasture, wanting to get her to eat out of his hand. We had a "creep feeder" for the foals, one that was built so the babies could get in but the mares couldn't, and we kept it filled with tasty and nutritious growth feeds the foals really liked. Bill thought that if he got some of that feed the foal would eat out of his hand, figuratively and literally. He got some feed, then stood between the feeder and the baby, thinking she would get the idea.

Apparently she didn't want to cooperate, and kept trying to get around him. He would move to stay in front of her, outstretched hands full of feed, squatting down to be on her level. She put up with his attentions for some time, but as Judy and I watched we could see her getting more restless, and Bill had to be more agile to stay between the filly and the feeder where she wanted to be.

We warned him that the baby had had enough, but he wanted to keep trying. He didn't have a rope or halter on her, but kept moving around to block her path, wanting her to eat from his hands. He can be really persistent—doing retakes until it is done right seems to be second nature to him. It seemed to us that the filly was getting really tired of all this attention, but he kept on.

As the filly dodged to try to get around him, Bill shuffled over to block her path, when suddenly the filly whirled and kicked out, rear hooves catching Bill right in the crotch, then she trotted off happily into the pasture. Bill dropped the feed, scrambled over the pasture fence, collapsed on the ground, and just sat there for a few minutes with a really distressed look on his face, which turned to a wry smile as he started to chuckle, realizing the filly had educated him instead of the other way around.

Chapter 54
Blue Eyes

Since we were raising cow horses, with an emphasis on cutting and reining work, we continually were trying to get those that carried the instincts relating to working a cow. One of the old-time sires of really good horses that met that criteria is Old Granddad, descended from the great sire, King.

We were fortunate enough to find a mare that was only three years old that was a granddaughter of Old Granddad, named King's Waspy Gal. We purchased the mare even though she was a little taller than we preferred, but we liked her solid black color. She was not trained, but we figured she would make a good broodmare.

At this time, Mr. Gunsmoke was a leading sire of performance horses in reining and cutting, and his stud fee was about at the top of our program, at $5,000. His foals were constantly winning or placing high in cow horse competitions, but one flaw in his breeding program was that he was so brightly colored, sorrel with a big blaze and four white stockings, that often he threw "crop-outs" or foals not eligible to be registered by the AQHA because they had too much white. This reduced the value of the foal. We figured the solid black of Waspy would mask the tendency to have too much white. Any serious horse breeder knows that each mating is a gamble; producing a foal is not always possible, and if one comes along, there is no way to know what that baby will look like or what abilities it will inherit. Still, we felt it worth the gamble to breed the mare to Mr. Gunsmoke, so that was done. Eleven months later we were anxiously waiting for her to deliver. We watched her almost constantly, checking on her several times a night, each moment trying to visualize this beautiful, athletic baby we planned on.

One day I was at the barn doing some chores in the late morning, when suddenly I became aware that Waspy was pacing agitatedly around the corral, and suddenly she ran through the door into the foaling stall just over the divider from where I was. I watched as she trotted around the stall, went to the middle, lay down, and in a matter seconds had produced a foal. I was so astounded, and gratified, to see the foal born, and to be the onlooker as, unaided, it learned to stand up and nurse. It seemed a healthy foal, a filly, dark bay in color with a little stripe of white on its face — exactly the color we wanted.

However, there are other factors in the development of a horse besides the color of its coat, and as the baby grew we realized that instead of growing into the squat, broad, muscled, athletic shape of a cutting horse, it was looking more and more like a gangly, too-long in the legs (and especially the nose) baby moose. To top off the caricature, the eyes took on the light blue color some paint horses have. This, in concert with the long legs, made it almost impossible to take seriously anything the foal did, as it seemed more like a clown than a cow horse.

Obviously, we were really disappointed, and sold the foal as a yearling at a no-profit price. Soon we sold the mother, too. It was just another lesson in life, pointing out again that kids may or may not favor their parents in the areas that are important to those in charge. I do remember, though, that Waspy was a perfect mother, and raised a very healthy foal — the blindness of love does work in all societies.

Chapter 55
Why Bird Dogs Smell

Everybody who has owned a bird dog understands the multiple meanings of this title. Yes, bird dog instincts allow them to use their nose to greet visitors, friends, enemies and others; help the hunter find and flush birds; locate and retrieve downed game; and to prowl their territory to protect it from intruders.

However, the other way they smell is the topic of this page. If you have owned a free-roaming bird dog, you probably have experienced at the return from an outdoor excursion an offensive aroma picked up somewhere and happily carried home with the pet. The smell seems to permeate the coat, breath, paws, and especially the back of the neck, where I love to scratch, and then my hand smells also. Rufus was especially good at finding these smells, and managed to bring them home all too often.

To determine where the offensive aroma started, I began watching Rufus more closely as we worked around the ranch, or did anything together. It took a while, but one day I saw him rubbing his neck and back on the grass, writhing in apparent happiness, all four feet in the air, and I thought, "How cute, he's like a miniature bear, scratching on the ground." As he got up and trotted happily off in his daily wanderings, I walked over to where he had been scratching and looked closely at the ground. Instead of sweet-smelling crushed grass and clover, I saw the greasy, foul-smelling remains of a dead squirrel.

From that time I watched more closely, and found that he loved to roll or rub in not just dead things, but anything that smelled strongly, such as nearly fresh horse or cow manure.

Then I found the same action in fox dung, which he loved to eat, as well as rub in. He would quit doing those things when I yelled at him, but didn't seem to get the idea that he needed to refrain in the future. Well, that answered the "what", but did little for the "why" of his action.

Again, it's the bird dog instincts controlling behavior. When the far-back ancestors of Rufus (and other bird dogs) had to hunt and catch their meals or go hungry, the techniques of concealment and surprise were paramount. If he was out hunting and smelled like a pile of yesterday's goat dung, the goat being pursued was probably not as wary of that aroma on the wind as it would be at the aroma of a predator, and apparently those predators who mastered these arts were those who survived through the ages.

I've tried over the years with all my dogs to break them of this habit, and never succeeded. Instincts seem to be much stronger than training, or retraining. It's one of the inconveniences of life, I guess, to put up with more frequent bathing or other deodorizing. As with some other inconveniences, it's worth it.

Chapter 56
Publicity Shots

One beautiful spring day William Shatner came to visit the ranch, followed by a reporter and a photographer from *People Magazine*. Bill announced that they wanted to do an article that included some photos of him riding, and he wanted to ride Dandy, the really good looking ranch gelding. We thought that was a fine idea, but cautioned Bill that Dandy hadn't been ridden much recently and he may be feeling a little frisky. Then Bill said, "I'd like to ride bareback, let's not saddle him." Reluctantly I agreed.

Bill mounted up and rode Dandy down the road past the barn, then turned around and trotted up for the photographer. The photographer asked that this be repeated, then again. This was fine for Bill, he was used to retakes, and was really enjoying the rides, but Dandy didn't understand the why of the energetic trips to nowhere. It seemed to him that they should be going farther, or at the very least, *somewhere*. Judy and I could see Dandy getting quite agitated, but Bill didn't seem to mind. He was keyed in to the camera, not to the horse. We warned him that this was probably enough, that Dandy was too edgy to continue, but he asked for one more trip.

As they approached the barn on a brisk trot, Dandy apparently thought it would be better if they could cover more ground and get this nonsense over with, so he broke into a canter. That felt so good to him that he let his powerful hind quarters give an extra strong thrust or two and Bill came unattached. He landed not at all gracefully on his back on the road, and the reporter and the photographer loved it.

When the next issue of *People* magazine came out, it had the promised article, including a photo of Bill on his back in the road. The truth was ignored in the photo caption, however, that told how much Bill enjoyed doing his own stunt work. Such is Hollywood.

Chapter 57
Revising a TJ Hooker Script

While Bill was filming for the "TJ Hooker" series, his time was limited, but he still managed to occasionally visit the ranch. One weekend visit included his two Doberman dogs, two that had little exposure to country living and had spent very little time outside a kennel, and probably none off a leash. He took them for a tour of the ranch, introduced them to our dog, Rufus, and they got along okay.

That afternoon Bill spent some time in his house and left the dogs free to run outside, since Rufus lived outside and was fine. When he came out he called the dogs, but nobody came. We heard him calling, and asked where the dogs were, as Rufus was at the house, as usual. He had no idea, so we began scouring all the pastures, looking and calling. We looked in literally every possible location, knowing they were not country dogs, but not imagining they would leave with Bill there. We crossed the south fence and went up the hill above Grouse Creek, but still no sign of his Dobermans. When it came time for evening chores, I took care of the horses and then we looked some more.

Bill was getting really distraught. He had heard stories of pets traveling cross country for amazing distances to get home, and didn't want to think he would have to wait days or weeks for his dogs to return. We went to the east pasture, then to the place next door, where no one was home. Still he called; still no answering bark or happy dog. Then, on a whim, we looked in a wood shed beside the house on the neighboring ranch, and there, cowering in apparent fear of the wide open spaces of the out-of-doors, were the city-bred dogs. They seemed as glad to see Bill as he was to find them, and they happily went home. All was well again, we thought.

Next time Bill came to the ranch, he asked if we had watched the episode of "Hooker" that was filmed the week after the dog incident. It seems that somewhere in our scouring the hillsides looking for the missing Dobermans Bill had gotten in some poison oak, and his arm broke out in a big rash. Delaying filming of "Hooker" was not an option, so the screen writers made up a story of how Bill had injured his arm (sorry, I don't remember the details of that story) and he appeared with the arm covered in a bandage. Hollywood can adjust, if necessary.

Dalan, Judy, Marcy, and Bill on Dandy, 1981

Chapter 58
A Missing Baby

It was spring again, and all the mares were foaling, including the Saddlebreds. We brought one Saddlebred mare into the foaling corral between the house and the barn where we could watch her more closely. I would check on her all through the night, and a couple of days later when I got up in the morning she seemed agitated, striding around the pen. As I watched her, it occurred to me that she didn't look pregnant anymore, she was suddenly thin again. There was no baby in the pen, no other signs of a birth, yet the mare had definitely foaled. I recalled some whinnying in the night, but when I had got up then and checked, all seemed normal. One of the quarter horse mares in the pasture across a lane was showing undue interest in all of this, trotting up and down the fence, but that in itself wasn't unusual at foaling time, so I had gone back to bed.

A quick look in the pen, and then a trip around the ranch showed no signs of a baby. All the obvious conclusions were brought up and discounted (mountain lions, etc.) and there was still no reason for a baby horse to just disappear. I looked for tracks in the dusty road. I checked the fence again. I reexamined the mare. Nothing made any sense. I leaned on the fence and just stood there, trying to think of something. Nothing came to mind except how were we going to explain to Bill that this mare wasn't really pregnant and didn't foal at all? In disgust I just left the corral and walked around the house to get away from the thought of these problems for a while.

Behind the house grows a large pine tree and assorted shrubbery. One of the large, thick shrubs, taller than I am, grows right next to the board fence of the main pasture. For some reason I walked over to the fence by that shrub and as I reached out to lean on the fence, saw movement by the shrub. What?—there, lodged in between the bushy shrub and the board fence was a skinny little hind end of a horse. Moving the brush aside, I pushed through to the front of the little backside, put my arm around its neck, and backed out a newborn foal. It had traveled along the fence until the branches of the shrub stopped it and it just didn't know how to back out of where it was.

Apparently the mare had foaled next to the fence on the downhill side of the pen, and the baby had rolled underneath. From there it had followed along the fence next to the other mare in the pasture across the lane until it got stuck in the "no reverse gear" mode behind the bush. It took a while to get the mother to accept it back, but after some work she did, and all was well. Yes, I did block off the space under the bottom fence board so that it could not happen again.

Chapter 59
A Friendly Wave

Three Rivers is a friendly place, and was even more so a few years back when everybody knew almost everyone else. It was important that we waved or otherwise acknowledged the neighbors as we traveled up and down the road, keeping in touch even though we didn't always stop to visit.

One early morning as I was driving down the hill I saw Jim Wells out in the front pasture on a young horse he had been training, getting experience on the colt, as that is the only way to season a young horse and make it into a reliable mount. As I passed by, I stuck my arm out the window of the truck and waved merrily. Jim's reaction, as expected, was to throw one arm up in a corresponding wave of neighborliness, taking his mind off the horse he was riding and grinning a greeting.

The colt, inexperienced as it was, didn't understand the dual release of Jim's mind and one of his hands, let alone the reason for one of Jim's arms to be flung in the air, and figured this was a time to flee and unload that burden from its back. It took a huge jump forward and started bucking through the pasture, with Jim hanging on and trying to regain control, his long legs wrapping around the horse's body and his hands trying to get the colt's head up from the ground. It took a few jumps before settling down, and all was well again.

I saw Jim a few days later, and he said, "I am going to consider whether to wave at you or not when you go past." I laughed and thanked him for the show, saying that I wouldn't charge him for the advanced training of the colt he was riding. He grinned, recognizing that he had had a lesson in riding lessons, that of keeping your mind on what is going on with the horse, rather than letting it wander. As the old cowboy adage states, "Keep your mind in the middle and a leg on each side."

Chapter 60
Talented Rufus

Rufus was the first dog Judy and I had. We raised him from a puppy, and with no other dogs around. We felt this taught him more human things, and made a much more obedient dog. There are those who say an animal doesn't think, but we know they do. Some of these theories about behavior must be written by those who have little first-hand experience with the intelligence of someone like Rufus.

Rufus learned so much English that it was scary. After we moved to Three Rivers he was our only dog again, and became even more attached to us and more educated. He fit right in to the summer routine at the river, enjoying the cool water and the warm rocks. Judy smoked cigarettes then, and one day at the river she realized coming out of the swimming hole that she had left her cigarettes on the other side of the river. She simply looked at Rufus and said, "Go bring me my cigarettes." I was rather startled at this, because when Rufus crossed the river he jumped lustfully into the water to get the full cooling effect, drowning anything in his mouth.

I couldn't see how this would do anything but soak the cigarettes, except to cool off the dog. Rufus looked at her a moment, jumped into the river, swam across, got out the other side and picking up the pack, walked gently this time into the water, and holding his head as high as he could to keep his parcel dry, swam back with his delivery, his gentle mouth bringing it unharmed to her.

We decided it was a fluke, but a few days later as Judy was helping the farrier with the horses she found she had left her pack at the barn, some distance from where they were trimming hooves. She told Rufus to "get my cigarettes" and he promptly trotted off and delivered them.

Her lighter had been beside, but not attached, and she said, "go get my lighter, too," and he trotted off again and was soon back with the lighter. The farrier stood open-mouthed at this performance and later told everyone all over his route about the miraculous dog the Smiths had.

Bird dogs get old, just like all of us do, and after a few years at the ranch in Three Rivers we began to realize how old Rufus was. He had come with us from Idaho, and had enjoyed a wonderful, full life. When his life was over, we wanted him to be part of the ranch, so I picked a special place on the Grouse Creek side of the pasture, and buried him there. I used the tractor to move a big, granite rock over the top of his grave and then chiseled an "R" into the face of it.

Many years later, Sal Natoli, a caretaker of the ranch, asked me about a big rock that he had discovered in the lower pasture that had an "R" chiseled into its side. He was pleased to know the story of Rufus.

I learned from Rufus that if you really want to be of service to someone, there is a way to accomplish that, even if it's something you shouldn't know how to do.

Judy and Rufus at the swimming hole, 1979

INTERIM PERIOD II

Chapter 61
Not-So-Wily Coyote

One of my favorite walks has been and still is along the Twin Lakes Canal near my boyhood home in southern Idaho. There is always a concentration of wildlife in the area, sometimes something to hunt or fish for, sometimes something that just entertains. On one of our holiday visits to the old family farm, our daughter, Terry and I were out enjoying an afternoon walk that led us to the top of the tunnel hill into Water Hollow. The soft ground made walking noiseless, the wind in our faces blew our scent behind us, and as we crested the top of the ridge, there was a coyote standing just down the other side, not more than fifty feet away. He had no idea there was anyone else around, and was staring intently across to another ridge, probably watching for a rabbit or other lunch item.

I motioned to Terry to be quiet, and we took a few more steps. Still he focused on whatever had his attention as we came within about fifteen yards. We stopped, watched a few seconds, then I shouted loudly, "HEY!"

It looked as if the poor, startled coyote had springs in his legs. He vaulted what seemed like two feet in the air, twisted his head around while still gaining elevation to see what was there, landed with legs already in "run extra fast" motion and took off down the hill.

Terry and I chuckled all afternoon as we recounted the speed with which poor Not-So-Wiley had left the area. Focusing on your goal is imperative if you are to get anywhere, but it may also be prudent to be aware of things that may walk up on you from the direction you least expect.

Chapter 62
Demonstration of Muscle

All of us dream of being stronger, speaking temporally or spiritually, but often we wonder how to accomplish this evasive goal. I learned a few years ago that we can do what we need to do, if we only have the right mindset.

Judy and I were traveling one early morning toward Star Valley, Wyoming, when we saw a large bull moose coming down the other side of the canyon toward the highway, looking like he was in a traveling mood. I decided I knew where he would cross the road if he was going to, made a U-turn, and parked along the side of the highway just down the hill from the anticipated crossing. As is true of many of the roads in that area, there was a long gap in traffic, and no other vehicles came along. In a couple of minutes an impressive set of antlers poked up over the lower bank of the road about 75 yards from us, followed by that distinctive, long, homely nose, and then the gangly but powerful body of the moose. As he climbed onto the roadbed he gave us a cursory glance and walked purposefully across the pavement.

The upper bank of the roadway was nearly straight up for four or five feet, then a barbed wire fence was set back a bit from the edge, and the hill continued with quite a steep slope upward. As the traveler approached this bank, he stepped up and started to climb it as if it were no obstacle at all to him. Just as he reached the top of the bank, his antlers caught on the top wire of the fence and he stopped.

Have you ever watched a big bulldozer dig its blade in and seem to become part of the earth as it strains with the load? This was the thought that came to my mind as the body of the moose settled toward the ground, muscles obviously bunching for maximum power, and all his concentration focusing on what was delaying his progress up the hill.

To my surprise, he simply raised his antlers, the top wire broke, and he stepped over the other wires and walked up the hill as if nothing had happened. After he had disappeared over the ridge, I got out and examined the fence and the trail. The top barbed wire was cleanly broken, and the tracks approaching the fence were deep in the earth.

As I thought about this extraordinary event, I decided that there were some lessons of benefit here. First, he didn't see the obstacle of the wire fence as something that would stop his journey, but merely a slight delay. Next, he knew his strength was sufficient to take care of what was holding him back and with his mind fixed firmly on the goal of cresting the next ridge it was no problem to deal with the wire. As we travel the path of life, we need more of the attitude of that homely but beautiful animal, whose motto seemed to be "The difficult we do right away, the impossible just takes a little bit longer."

(Photo courtesy of Kelleen Smith)

Chapter 63
First Hollow

Each family farm seems to have one or more areas that hold magic for our minds. For me, First Hollow was, and still is, one of these places. It is around the hill toward the far west end of the farm, and being so remote seems to attract more wild things, plus it takes some time to hike to, thus allowing the mind to rid itself of other thoughts and become receptive to the spirit of the place. Also, it is quite open to the view, yet has good grass and a grove of cottonwoods and willows in the deep canyon below the canal. Above the canal is mostly sage brush, which makes good open viewing for spotting deer or jackrabbits. Much earlier, when I was maybe four, Dad came rushing in the house looking for the camera, and for me. He loaded me on his shoulders and headed for First Hollow. At the edge of the cottonwood grove there was a big willow branch arched over the trail, and on it sat two baby owls, big enough to get out of the nest, but too young to fly. He posed me under them, took a photo, and we quietly left them to their development.

The author in First Hollow, ca. 1943

On the lower part of the canal bank sat a relic of the building of the canal, a poured-concrete roller about four feet in width and nearly that in diameter. This had a heavy steel rod through the center for an axle, and was used to compact the fill dirt as the canal was built. It was a welcome sight for over forty years anytime I walked past, reminding me of how hard our grandfather and others worked to provide irrigation water for their own land and the downstream farmers. It became a fixture in our minds as well as in the hollow area.

The roller resting in First Hollow, 1972

Much later I was living in a neighboring valley (Bear Lake) and drove over to visit the old farm. As I traveled up the hollow toward the canal I met my younger sisters on one of their walks and stopped to visit.

They asked if I knew if the roller was still in First Hollow, as they hadn't seen it as they walked past. The canal maintenance people were working with a large backhoe and a bulldozer, cleaning the canal, so they had hurried past, but had missed seeing our old friend. I hurriedly drove around the canal bank road to near where it should have been, but couldn't see the roller. I parked the truck and walked to the construction area. Going to where I remembered the roller to have been sitting, I looked closely at the new piles of dirt that had been pushed out of the canal, and saw the end of the axle shaft just barely sticking out of the side of a pile.

One of the equipment operators was a neighbor I had known all my life, Bryce Egley, and I waved for him to stop the dozer. I asked about the roller, and he said that he and the backhoe operator had seen it, but didn't know if it was important to anyone. I suggested that we do something other than bury it, and the backhoe operator said he thought his equipment was big enough to lift it out. A scoop or two cleared the way and a deft maneuver with the bucket brought the roller to the surface and set it safely on the undisturbed part of the road.

Bryce volunteered that he had a flatbed trailer that would haul it if I wanted to use it, and I drove to his farm, hooked up the trailer and came back. The backhoe set the roller on the trailer, I strapped it down and took it to the family park on the river, where it resides today. Special memories are worth saving.

Chapter 64
The Grass is Always Greener?

There seems to be a built-in dissatisfaction in each of us about our lives and our position in society that tends toward wanting something different from what we already have. If this impetus is directed in a positive way it can motivate us to improve ourselves in our occupation or our knowledge, but if not carefully guided it can become no more useful than idle chatter, leading to wasted time and useless envy.

When Judy and I were living in Paris, Idaho we saw a perfect example of the effects of the old saying, "The grass is always greener on the other side of the fence." We were driving home during the height of the spring snowmelt runoff, and many of the low-lying fields and pastures were flooded. Ovid Creek, in particular, was out of its banks and covering two pastures with up to a foot or two of clear, cold water. A herd of Holstein cows was wandering through the shallows, feeding on the remnants of left-over fall grasses, as the spring growth had not yet started. The tendency of this variety of cattle to try everything on the other side of the fence is legendary, as those who have tried to keep them penned up know very well.

Holstein cows in an Ovid pasture

As we traveled past the pasture, we looked out at the cows and saw one that was thirsty and had stopped to drink—no need to walk to a drinking place, as they were all standing in the flood. This particular cow was on the edge of the herd, near a fence that divided the two pastures. Instead of just putting her head down to drink, she moved over to the fence and carefully inserted her head between the barbed wires, then drank from "the other side of the fence," where it obviously, for her, tasted best. Never mind that it was the same water for a couple hundred feet in all directions, it was a stolen sip from someone else's pasture.

As we chuckled at her placing herself in a precarious position in the barbed wire fence to accomplish what she foolishly thought was best, we couldn't help but compare that to the lives of humans that overlook accomplishments and blessings they already have in favor of seeking something else with no more purpose than someone else owns it or it is something they have never owned or done.

Chapter 65
The Abundance Mentality

The basis of building a good relationship in a marriage or a friendship is what is known as the Abundance Mentality, the belief that there are plenty of rewards out there, that my winning is not at the expense of someone else. Many people are deeply scripted in the Scarcity Mentality. They see life as having only so much, as though there were only one pie out there, and if someone were to get a big piece of the pie, it would mean less for everybody else. People with this Scarcity Mentality have a very difficult time sharing recognition and credit, power or profit—even with those who help in the production of the same. They also have a very hard time being genuinely happy for the successes of other people—even and sometimes especially, members of their own family or close friends and associates. It's almost as if something is being taken from them when someone else receives special recognition or windfall gain or has remarkable success or achievement.

It's difficult, wrote Stephen Covey, for a person with a Scarcity Mentality to be a member of a complementary team, or a synergistic marriage. The Abundance Mentality, on the other hand, flows out of a deep inner sense of personal worth and security. It builds on the belief that there is plenty of everything out there and enough to spare for everybody. It results in sharing of prestige, of recognition, of compliments, of decision making. It opens possibilities, options, alternatives, and creativity in all relationships.

A person who has character rich in integrity, maturity, and the Abundance Mentality has a genuineness that goes far beyond technique, or lack of it, in human interaction. These traits are especially valuable in the closeness of a marriage, where many times communication is unsaid, but deeply felt.

The trust generated by this attitude eliminates the negative energy normally focused on differences in personality and creates a positive, cooperative energy focused on thoroughly understanding the issues and resolving differences in a mutually beneficial way.

The bird dogs in my life have been, without exception, of the Abundance Mentality, and have been happiest when we all win together.

Chapter 66
Drivers

One of the benefits of living in several locations in several states is that we got to know idiosyncrasies of the inhabitants of these areas. Some were simply interesting, such as the Bear Lake County, Idaho, speech inflections that cause the natives to say, for instance, "Were you barn in a born?"

Another trait that shows up is the driving habits of different areas. Perhaps these differences are not as pronounced now as they once were, but it seems to me that the drivers in different states have particular tendencies in their driving. For instance, the following traits seem to show up:

Drivers in California are compelled to pass the vehicle immediately ahead of them.

Drivers in Idaho will allow you to drive on their road if you don't get in their way.

Drivers in Utah drive as if the posted speed is the legal minimum.

Chapter 67
Fishing Practice

Anything worth doing is worth doing right, the old saying says, and fishing is included in this. To be good at it requires practice, and I got plenty of practice, plus good coaching, when I was young. Undoubtedly the best practice sessions were those when my dad and I would catch literally a washtub full of Rocky Mountain whitefish, in the evenings when the surface of the river just boiled with activity, the kind of times that fly fishermen dream about but seldom see. I seemed to forget how essential that kind of learning is as much later in life I took my daughter Carolyn and her family on a fishing trip.

We had decided on a little recreational fishing, the kind that is just for the fun of catching fish, lots of them, and the Oneida Reservoir had always provided lots of fish and fun. We were catching some panfish and enjoying releasing them, when I heard a loud splashing out on the water. I looked, and a rainbow trout, probably sixteen inches long, was thrashing on the surface, trying to get loose from something. I turned to see what was on the other end and saw granddaughter Karis frantically reeling, pole pointed straight out, and backing up the beach trying to land the fish that was too big to be handled that way. It was only a moment, though it seemed longer, especially to Karis, before the line broke and the fish disappeared into the lake.

I was disappointed, but Karis was devastated, and I realized that if Karis had been properly taught how to "play" a large fish until it wears out and is manageable, she would have landed the fish of the day. I felt so bad for her.

It occurred to me that this would be a good time to practice landing large fish, and I knew where to make that happen.

Just over the hill, in the community of Mink Creek, Vernon Keller had a series of ponds fed by Birch Creek, and he had stocked them with rainbow trout some years earlier Many of these trout were now huge. He allowed fishing, for a fee, and it seemed to me that adequate practice was a good reason to pay a fee. We loaded up and drove to Vernon's ponds.

It was only a matter of minutes until everyone was catching, playing, and landing large trout, and the practice got really serious when Reese, the young grandson, then probably ten or so, learned how to fly fish in this one session. He had the mindset that it takes to be a successful fly fisherman. This mindset seems to be inherited, not acquired, and like the instincts of a good bird dog, just needs a little directing, then the autonomic functions take over and it works like magic.

Reese had spotted, at the upper end of one of the pools, a trout of probably five or six pounds lying in the current of the inflow and lazily feeding on insects that floated past. He had determined that he would catch that fish. He cast his fly to the fish, but it wouldn't bite, and he tried over and over with the same result. We stayed nearby, but allowed him room to do his solitary thinking about how to make the reluctant rainbow trout cooperate. Seldom have I seen the kind of determination I saw in Reese as he would sit on the bank and think, then get up and cast his fly to the fish, be ignored, sit and think some more, change his fly pattern, cast again, get no results, but not give up.

We were each doing our own thing, enjoying catching and releasing fish, forgetting about Reese and his problem, when I heard the loud splash of a hooked fish. There was Reese, fly rod bent nearly double, properly playing the trout he had been stalking, and I lent a hand only to net the large fish and remove the barbless hook before watching it swim lazily away.

Reese was so proud, but no more than his grandfather was, as he became a full-fledged fly fisherman with the outsmarting of that fish. Later on that trip he showed how much he had learned as we successfully fished for wild trout in mountain streams and he did well there, too.

His sister, Karis, also showed that she could hook, play, and land those large trout, and if she had had the chance to do the practice first, there could have been a much more satisfactory result on the Oneida Reservoir trout. Practice does, indeed, make for perfect performance.

THE "CHIP" ERA

Chapter 68
Choosing a Bird Dog

I wasn't sure I was ready for another dog, as I worked long hours (a hazard of the self-employed) and too many of those were out of town. It just didn't seem that I would be able to arrange the time to spend with a young dog that it takes to establish a meaningful training relationship. Judy, on the other hand, seemed to sense that the time was right for us to expand our family, speaking in a bird dog way of course. She reasoned that if we got a puppy now it would be over that stage of knocking us down by the time we were old enough for that to be a problem. Also she was home much of the time, so she could give it the attention we both knew it needed.

It wasn't long before she found an ad in the local newspaper for a litter of nearly eight-week old pups. The mother was a chocolate lab that escaped her kennel one night and the father a neighborhood German shorthair pointer that was happy to see her out of confinement — a perfect Smith bird dog pedigree as far as we were concerned.

A drive to a neighboring town was a nice way to spend an afternoon, Judy said, and I owed her some attention, so consented to drive us there. She had called ahead for an address, and we arrived not long after lunch. The puppies, eight or ten of them, were let out in front of the house to play, and we sat down with their owner to watch.

Two were colored much like our former dog, Rufus — dark brown with some white on the face and a white tip on the tail. One of these also had white feet and underside with shorthair-type speckles of brown.

All the pups played back and forth across the front of the house, from the front porch across to the end of the house and back. There was a large, shallow bowl of water on the edge of the driveway, and they could stop to drink if they wanted, though not many took the time for that.

As they trooped across the driveway, each would trot around the water dish, except for one. The male with the speckles on his feet would follow the group along the wall, but instead of turning out around the water dish would step right in it, splashing loudly, then jump on out and follow along. He was the only one to do this, and it caught my attention right away. I just sat and watched for several revolutions of this game, and he never missed splashing through the water dish, and was the only one that did this.

One of the most enjoyable things to me is to have a dog that loves the water, not just for hunting ducks, but for throwing things to retrieve and just to keep cool in the summer heat, so I watched the speckle footed one closely, growing more and more interested in his very evident personality. He seemed to get along well with the group, and was not the leader or the last to move, but was always there. The thing that stood out the most in contrast to the others was his apparent attraction to the water.

We must have watched them for an hour or more, and by then I was no longer an uninvolved chauffer to my wife, but an eager participant in this game of deciding which puppy would give us the most pleasure, and fit in best with our lifestyle. When I finally forced myself to make a decision, the order of conclusions came like this: it was time to have a new dog, the right one was probably here, and it was the one with the speckled feet. We took him home, and he became everything we had desired, especially an excuse to spend more time doing things other than working. From the start Chip was a benefit to our lives.

Chapter 69
Watermelon Chip

Everyone has heard stories of the soft-mouthed bird dog. Chip was still quite young, really still a pup, when he demonstrated how adept he was with his mouth. We had brought home a small watermelon, probably eight or ten pounds, and had put it at the bottom of the outside stairway to the basement, as that was a nice, cool place to store it.

It was the next afternoon that I looked out on the back lawn and saw a watermelon sitting there. Now, that is funny, I thought, I hadn't moved the melon since bringing it home. I checked with Judy, and she hadn't moved it, either.

An examination of the melon offered some clues. There were a few small, round holes in the rind, but no damage to the melon. Nothing else seemed out of the ordinary. I looked at Chip, asked if he knew how the melon got there, and he hung his head and looked away, a sure sign that he understood what I was asking.

How he got his mouth to open so wide, yet still closing it enough to carry the melon up a flight of stairs is still beyond me, but there was no other explanation. Had he been so bored that he wanted a ball to play with? Had he just succumbed to the urge to move it because it could be done? How did he manage to lift the melon and carry it up the stairs? He has never repeated that feat.

Chapter 70
Grouse For Dinner

My bird dog, Chip, still loves to go in the truck, and when I was in the outdoor real estate business in Idaho it put me in the truck a lot, so I often had an excuse to offer him a day of riding. One day I had a late afternoon appointment to show a mountain property outside of Soda Springs, and it looked like a perfect opportunity to take Chip with me. Because it was grouse season, I brought the shotgun so after my real estate showing we could try to get a grouse to come home with us for dinner.

I honestly don't remember how the showing went, or who the real estate prospect was, or if he ever bought anything, but I do remember that Chip and I found where the grouse were staying that evening. We succeeded in bagging two fat ruffed grouse for Chip to fetch, and he was elated. It did require some time and quite a bit of hiking, as well as the customary mad dash to retrieve when the gun went off, so by dark we were both pretty tired out, but very happy and satisfied. I loaded the happy dog in the back of the truck and threw the grouse in with him, as always. The ride home had always been nap time for him after a workout like we just had, especially as darkness had now taken over. The shell on the truck gave him shelter from the wind, and there was a scrap of carpet on the floor for comfort.

A funny feeling invaded my thought time as we traveled down the mountain toward town, and when another vehicle came up behind me I looked in the mirror and in its lights I could see a silhouette of Chip standing up, with his head down, and he was moving around instead of lying down.

That was strange, and when we got to Soda Springs, I stopped for gas. I put the nozzle in the tank and then looked inside the shell to see what had been going on.

The truck bed was littered with grouse feathers, and on the edge of the area where I had put two grouse there lay one grouse, some feathers, and the feet and remnants of two lower legs from another grouse. The balance of that bird was totally missing. Obviously Chip was hungrier than I had ever known him to be, and we had missed supper time, so he fed himself.

The remaining grouse was not touched, so I told him he'd had enough and went in the store and bought us each a hamburger to eat as we drove home. When we arrived sometime later, the hamburger was gone and Chip was asleep. The remaining grouse lay where I had left it, untouched.

Although Chip and I traveled many times after that with him sharing the truck space with various bagged game, he never touched another one. It would seem that the lesson had been learned.

Chapter 71
Internal Clock

Chip has a remarkable clock. He doesn't carry it on his collar or in his mouth, but it definitely exists, and it is exceptionally accurate.

Judy and I can be reading, working, watching a movie or napping, paying absolutely no attention to Chip or what he is doing, and when it comes one o'clock in the afternoon (time for a snack of dog bones) or five o'clock (time for evening feeding) suddenly he is in our face, wagging his tail expectantly and looking really interested in getting our attention. Sometimes he fudges a little and tries to get us to feed him a few minutes early, but quickly gives in when we say, "No, it's not time, Chip." When those few minutes have passed and it is time, there he is, tail wagging and ears at attention.

The most interesting thing about this clock is that it resets to daylight saving time, or standard time, just like my computer does. Chip doesn't have a visible antenna, but apparently he does have a hard drive that is connected to something out there somewhere, or to something in there somewhere. Over the years I've become convinced that my dog can not only read my mind, but can arrive at my conclusions before I do, and be waiting there when I finally arrive, wagging his tail and wondering where I've been. I guess this connection he has also sets his feeding clock.

Nine o'clock p.m. is the time for a last trip out before spending the night in the house. If he is invited out much earlier, he just looks at us. If we miss that time, he has a tendency to stand up, shake, and stretch casually, then look at each of us in turn as if to say, "Did you forget something?"

In the morning, if I get up earlier than usual for some reason, he will stay asleep, or at least curled up and resting, until I say "Time to go feed the horses," at which he will do his famous casual stretch as he climbs out of bed and joins me for some outside time.

I look forward to the time when I can understand the clockworks of the canine world.

Chapter 72
Gift Fish for Breakfast

In 2001 Judy and I lived in the Jackson Hole, Wyoming area for about a year. The log cabin we rented in Wilson had a wonderful creek in the back yard.

The stream was a natural creek, not a man-made canal, and ran through a former gravel pit, a rather deep pond with a small island having some willows growing on it. A handful of dog food tossed on the water brought an almost instantaneous response from the resident cutthroat trout, showing they knew about and were used to enjoying a little feeding. Also, the island was home to a pair of nesting Canada geese, another great entertainment.

The goose family, Wilson, WY, 2001

One morning I was standing looking out the window watching the sun rise when suddenly the mother goose flew off her nest, splashed into the pond, and squawking loudly, flapped furiously toward the other bank. As she charged, a very startled great blue heron flew up from that edge of the pond and left for friendlier territory. The goose swam back to the island and climbed on the nest again. I guessed she was just worried about the safety of her nest, and didn't want the heron around.

It was only a few minutes later that Judy and I took our usual morning walk, and as we rounded the pond through a freshly cut alfalfa field I looked down and there on the ground was a 16-inch cutthroat trout. I am a lifetime fisherman, I know a "fresh" condition when I see a trout, and this one was definitely fresh. A quick examination showed a mark down each side just below the dorsal fin, where obviously the heron had grasped the fish, pulled it from the water, and lost it in the dash to escape the charging goose.

We knew the heron would not return to eat the fish, but didn't want it to go to waste, so we took it home for breakfast. It was excellent. I probably would not recommend a hungry fisherman follow a great blue heron around waiting for it to drop something, but this time it worked wonderfully, thanks to a nervous mother goose.

Chapter 73
Jackson Hole

Chip was still quite young when we moved to Jackson Hole, Wyoming to be near some building projects we had there. The place we had rented in Wilson, as I stated earlier, was out of town and had a nice stream running through the yard.

Even though it was pretty much by itself, we wanted Chip to learn to stay in the yard and not wander too far. We thought we were making good progress, when one morning a dog showed up just across the back fence, and Chip decided it was play time. He scampered under the wire fence and playfully bounded up to the dog, expecting to play, when the dog snarled and snapped at him, biting him on the lip. Chip was totally surprised, and quickly retreated into our yard. The dog stayed on the other side of the fence, and Chip got the idea immediately that he was safe on his side. It became very easy to keep him in the yard after that.

The Wilson cabin, 2001

Another distraction was the geese and the ducks that nested on the pond. Chip loved to watch them, especially from inside the house, where he could see them and they couldn't see him, and would come up on the lawn. We would talk gently to him, and he got the idea that they were on safe ground, for when we would be outside in the yard, he would just watch them. One day the mother duck brought eight or so ducklings right up on the lawn, within thirty feet or so of Chip, and he just quivered, he was so excited, but did not chase them.

Judy loved to take Chip on walks along the country roads, even in the winter. The stream was spring fed, and was warm enough that it would not freeze over. The ducks would stay all year, feeding in the shallows and resting in the deeper pools. One day as Judy walked with Chip she saw a flock of ducks fly in and land in a pool, and Chip saw them, too. He bolted across the snow bank and disappeared. "Oh, no," thought Judy, "what if he catches one?"

She hardly had the thought when Chip appeared, proudly carrying a duck in his mouth. "Now what do I do?" she said to herself, and as Chip brought his catch to her, she saw it was still alive. She asked him to drop it, he did, and it disappeared back over the snow bank into the river bed. Chip seemed happy to be able to make a retrieve, but wanted nothing further. This is another of those times that I've wondered what goes on in his head—how he adjusts to our way of thinking.

Chapter 74
Cultural Differences

When Judy rides her horse, Chip loves to go, following or leading, always moving, checking with his nose everything that is or was along the trail. He ranges to both sides of the trail, forward mostly, as if his job was to clear the way for the riders to come along.

When Kathleen McCleary rides with Judy and brings her dogs, a different pattern comes into play. Those two dogs seem to be more into themselves, running far and wide, disappearing for sometimes hours, then showing up again unexpectedly, maybe just in time to load up and go home. Since they are of cattle dog breeding, they can be useful for clearing the trail when the pasture cattle or horses are slow to move out of the way. If other groups of riders or hikers have dogs, Kathleen's dogs bark at the newcomers, as if to express their rights to the trail, while Chip is quiet.

Chip acts differently when Kathleen's dogs are along on the ride. He stays near to Judy and her horse, as if to let the other dogs do the checking of the trail, and doesn't run as far away. Sometimes he is actually right in front of her horse, and a hazard to her horse's movement. At lunch time he is a real pest, wanting to be underfoot all the time. When other dogs show up, Chip is quiet, willing to get acquainted with the newcomers, but in a quiet, non-threatening way.

How these cultural differences are explained is a mystery to us. What are the changes in Chip's behavior, what is the mindset he assumes when the other dogs are present? Why does he feel such a need to be underfoot as opposed to running free? Why is his personality so different from the others? It is a pleasure to see these differences, and to know that each "person" in the group is truly an individual, with individual characteristics.

Chapter 75
Horses and Fences

For many years now I've kept horses, and I always seem to learn something from their actions. Today I watched out the window as two of them moved through the pasture, gently grazing and sniffing out new greenery to munch on. When they reached the far end of the pasture they turned to travel along the fence, still enjoying their morning snacks. I thought, "What if the fence weren't there, what would they do?"

Fences take many forms. Some are fancy white vinyl, some are post and pole, some are wire of one kind or another, but all are for the same purpose, that is, to keep something in or out; to define a boundary; to make a visual reference appear; or to claim ownership. In my case, they are for the safekeeping of my wife's horses, to let them know where they are allowed and where they are not. The fence tells them how far they can go, and turns them back if they desire to exceed that limit.

A fence is good only if it is honored, and in this we begin to learn lessons in behavior. As we watch how horses act with the fence, we can get an idea about human behavior as it relates to those limits and boundaries we need to learn to honor. Some horses seem to spend most of their time reaching through to get whatever treats are on the other side, caring little about the danger of being tangled up or whether the fence is damaged by the pressure. Indeed, some seem to sense that if they keep pressuring the fence it will loosen and allow them to reach farther, as indeed it does.

Other horses honor the fence, staying well within its limits. Obviously, these are our favorites, as their gentle nature, respectful attitude, and sense of obeying the rules engenders feelings of love, while those who continually test the limits stir up feelings of resentment—why do they act the way they do?

It's as if some are interested only in their own appetites and fulfillment of their own desires, while others, our favorites, honor the limits and rules established for their benefit.

What if the fence were to disappear when the horses approached it? Would there be danger from automobiles or other hazards? Would they wind up where there was not enough good feed? What about mistreatment of those who found them wandering and had no respect? Could they forget which way was home and feel lost and alone?

Why do we have limits and boundaries in our lives? For the same reasons that horses need fences. We don't have to ascribe these limits to a God or other authority, but they begin with a sense of decency about our interactions with others, as well as the respect we have for ourselves, our bodies and our general sense of well-being. Our fences should be kept well-tended and mended, tight and straight, shiny and bright as it were. We cannot pick and choose to honor some fences and ignore others. Obedience to rules brings liberty, not restriction.

We all have a conscience (though some of us have suppressed its activity to a level almost beyond recognition) and it will let us know when something is beyond a limit we should be honoring, if we but pause a moment to let it speak to us. Listen to these pronouncements, find your fences and the limits they define, stay morally firm, and watch your life improve.

An example of a horse and a fence

Chapter 76
Friendship

Chip always seems content to be alone with us, and we have no desire to own a second dog. Because we make him part of the family and treat him with respect and consideration, his natural loving nature teaches him to be respectful and considerate also. We have neighbors and friends with dogs, so he is exposed to other dogs socially, and gets along very well with them, but returns readily to us when the social visits are over. One of the real benefits of this kind of training and living in the country as we do is that we can let him run loose rather than keeping him locked in a kennel or pen all the time, including when we are gone for a few hours, and he stays at home.

When our near neighbors, Darryl and Sally Klocke, went on vacation a couple of years ago, they asked if we would let their dog, Shiloh, stay with us for ten days while they were away. Shiloh is an outside dog, well behaved, not prone to bark needlessly, and smiles (actually turns her lips back and shows her teeth, not threateningly, and wags her tail vigorously) whenever she sees someone she likes. We nicknamed her Smiley, and she answers to either name. Smiley came to stay with us while Darryl and Sally were gone, and was no trouble. When they came back, she went home and was happy. A while later they went again, the dog stayed with us again, and all was well.

It was some time after their return from this second absence that one day Smiley showed up unexpectedly at our house, played with Chip, then disappeared again.

We thought little of it, until she showed up again, and again. This time we had to call Sally to come pick her up and take her home. Then one day Smiley came over to visit Chip and wouldn't go home when night came. We didn't feed her, because we didn't want to make her feel like this was home. Wrong—she had adopted us, and stayed until we took her home the next day. A few hours later she was back.

Judy called Sally, and Sally took Smiley home again and locked her up. Nobody was very happy with that situation. After a discussion with Sally it was decided that Smiley was welcome to live on our back porch if that was what she wanted—Sally would bring over some food occasionally, and the dog would be everybody's dog. When I saw Darryl he would ask, "How is our dog?" Smiley and Chip played in the pasture, fast friends in the business of hunting ground squirrels and digging for gophers.

Smiley and Chip

Smiley stayed with us over a year, then one day a thunderstorm came past, and she was always scared of storms. She disappeared, and didn't show up for a day.

Judy finally called Sally, and learned that Smiley had showed up at their house on the day of the storm and she had locked her in the yard. Then Smiley adapted, and stayed, even when the gate was not locked. Not long after that, we moved back to Idaho, and Chip came with us, but Smiley stayed in Three Rivers. It was as if she knew there was a change coming, and she prepared for it by moving back home.

Chapter 77
A Parable by a Dog

A recent Sunday School lesson discussed the parable of the unjust judge and the widow (Luke 18:1-8). To summarize this, a hard-nosed judge is continually bothered by a widow who has a complaint against one she feels has wronged her. The judge tries to ignore her, but she keeps coming back until he finally says, "because this widow troubleth me, I will avenge her, lest by her continual coming she weary me."

The Lord's explanation of this is to show that God will take care of his children, even if not immediately, if they persist in asking for what they really need.

My bird dog, Chip, gives me daily a good portrayal of the parable of the unjust judge and the widow. My day begins with scripture reading and study for the Sunday School lesson. I like to do this sitting at the table in the breakfast nook, which has a window looking out on the rear deck. Chip spends time on that deck, not just because his bed is there, but also because the window is low enough that he can see inside. He sits on the deck and watches me as I read and study. He understands it may be some time before I come out to feed him, or go for a walk, or check on the horses, or move the pasture sprinklers, but I guess he figures he has no better activity than watching me to be sure he doesn't miss out on any one of these activities.

His gaze is more than steady—after a while it becomes intense, a force that cannot be ignored. He doesn't bark, or whine, or make any noise, but the energy generated by his locked-on focus reaches me despite my own concentration on what I am doing. I can ignore it for just so long, then I give in and get the outside activities of the day started so he can join me. When I come out the door and say, "Okay, let's go," he runs and jumps with pleasure as we travel together.

Nothing he does to get my attention is out of line, or an annoyance, or even slightly irritating—he just keeps pleasantly looking until my mind accepts his plea. This is the mindset, according to my understanding of the parable, that our Father in Heaven must want us to assume as we approach Him with our requests. Some prayers expressed just once or even more won't get an early answer, but must be worked on until solutions are resolved in our minds and hearts, and constantly, intently pled to Him who can—and will—make us capable of fulfilling these needs.

Chapter 78

A Medical Lesson

Today's lesson is one of patience and perseverance. Chip (our bird dog) is suffering from Valley Fever, a chronic disease that sometimes isn't curable, and also a weakened right shoulder. We don't know if they are directly related. The Valley Fever was probably picked up when Chip's nose was thrust into the dust of a squirrel hole, or when chomping down a mouse on his self-appointed pest control rounds.

The Valley Fever hasn't seemed to go away, even after about six months on an expensive medication. He still coughs, but has gained weight and has good coat condition. He loves to hunt, formally or just chasing things when we walk, and seems to have plenty of energy to do so, but when we return home he collapses into long naps. (Looks like a good life to me!) Sometimes he apparently hurts, and then is "sticky"—just doesn't want to do anything but cling to, or lean on, one of us. He doesn't want to be away from us, as Judy and I are his source of comfort.

His right shoulder is almost totally debilitated, with virtually no muscle left, yet when he forgets, in the heat of the chase, that it is so bad, he shows no limp or weakness. When a ground squirrel or gopher dives down its hole, Chip digs like a backhoe. Field mice are still a favorite snack, anytime. Yet, if we probe or pat his shoulder, he winces—he must be very sore.

The major change in the last few days is his attitude—more philosophical, quiet, perhaps even pensive; not keeping him from being enthusiastic about going on walks, but not anymore "frolicking" like a puppy. Is it just maturity? Not considering the speed at which the changes have come, I fear.

He still eats well, but again not enthusiastically, sometimes needs much coaxing to have his pill and food. When we start across the pasture, he will run ahead to see if any quail or squirrels need chasing, then when he gets too warm, will go for a swim in the river or pond. Again, when we get home he immediately drops to the floor and sleeps.

What lessons do I learn from him? He hurts, but doesn't whine, seems to know it doesn't help, and accepts that we are doing all we know how to do to make him as comfortable as possible. He leans on his friends for love and support, and always gives love, even when he hurts. He wants to do what he knows is right, including going on a hike when he's not really feeling like it. It must hurt to get in and out of the back of the truck, but he seems to realize that a little pain will be rewarded with a favorite ride, or a nap after—it's easy to forget that every pleasure has its price. When priming to jump in the truck, his concentration gets *so* intense, and from that I learn that we can often do more than is expected, or more than it appears we can, if we will just buckle down and really give it our all. Above all, he does not want to disappoint us, or feel like he is a burden. Love and consideration, independence, yet submitting to the ministrations of those who care for us and want to help—those are things we all must learn, and that it's sometimes easier to help others than accept the help of others, but both are a very important part of a good life.

(Update: Chip seems to have fully recovered from his illness, is off medication, has regained some of his lost muscle, bounces around like a puppy on cool mornings, and is happier than in a long time. It's good to have him back. He does, however, retain and exhibit what he learned of an increased capacity to love, and to share that love. Always a lesson for us in the way our bird dog friends live their lives, isn't there?)

Chapter 79
Adrenaline Rush

Last night (May 19, 2009) I procrastinated moving the last sprinkler in the pasture until after sundown. No reason, other than it was quite warm and I was tired from working all morning at the ranch and all afternoon at the Three Rivers Mercantile. When I finally got motivated to go out, I slipped on some sandals and strolled through the grass. I know there is always a possibility of snakes, especially this time of year when they are moving around to their summer dwelling places. Still, sandals are so comfortable, cool, and quick and easy to get on and off, and I'm always watching closely where I walk.

As I neared the sprinkler, it was not rotating, so I was distracted looking at it to see why. My step felt funny, so I looked down and protruding from under my sandal was the diamondback design of a large rattlesnake, writhing to get out of the weight I was putting on it.

The human mind can work so fast—in the next milli-millisecond, all these things (and more) went through my mind:
1) This is not a good thing; I need to be moved to anywhere else.
2) I am standing exactly on top of the snake's head—that is a good thing.
3) I still need to move, and <u>now</u>.
4) The coils of the body are going to be pushing on my ankle soon, and this may spring the head loose; that could be dangerous.
5) I am alone, it's a few hundred yards to the house and any help.
6) I think I heard a click or two, even though for years my deteriorating hearing hasn't been able to hear the buzz of the rattles.

7) What a healthy-looking body it has, probably an inch and a half in diameter in the middle, and maybe two and a half or three feet long!
8) Yes, that tail is vibrating, wish I could hear it.
9) Now, with no apparent thought, I am sailing backward through the air to safety.
10) Was that a four-letter word that came out of my mouth?

And as I landed and continued back-peddling, I saw the pasture grass moving as the snake headed the other way. I had no implements to do anything about it, so I took off for the house and better shoes. I put on heavy boots and returned and looked for it. Apparently it was as serious about leaving as I was—I didn't find it again.

I finished moving the sprinkler and went back to the house, still a little fidgety. I guess the Smith genetics (almost legendary fear of snakes) still live in all of us. Now that it's another day, I moved the sprinklers this morning with no problems—wearing my big heavy rubber boots, though. I keep a path mowed through the pasture to the garden, and stay on trails mostly. Judy didn't think it was very funny, but there is some humor, looking back from a safe distance. The snake was as anxious to be out from under my foot as I was to be away from him, and I don't think either of us wants to work on befriending the other.

The pasture where the meeting occurred

Chapter 80
Gyrations of Gratitude

One of the things we see missing too often in today's world is a feeling of gratitude—gratitude for all we have and gratitude for all we are and can become. In the words of the ancient Greek philosopher Epictetus, "He is a wise man who does not grieve for the things which he has not, but rejoices for those which he has." If our habit and attitude is to focus on the good things we have, rather than those things we lack, being happy is easier, and isn't that how we all want to be?

My list of things I am grateful for is too long for this missive, but I'll name some of them. I'm grateful for each of you who receive and read this anecdote. The opportunity to be a family, to have good friends, far outweighs the usual gifts of any season. My heart overflows with love for God, for His plan of salvation for each of us, for the part of that plan that generated the love of the Christmas season, and especially for that Savior (whose birth we commemorate as we symbolize it with gifts for those dear to us), the gift of His Son to us.

I am grateful, among other things, for books to read, music to hear, loving glances from those who mean much to me, the beauty of the earth and sky and sunshine and stars and clouds and grass and water and rocks and trees and flowers and fruit and fish. I'm so thankful to not have to settle for average, ordinary, or normal, when life can be so adventuresome and enjoyable. I am thankful that most of the time I don't feel much older than I did some 30 or 40 years ago, except that I definitely remember being faster and stronger, and perhaps more foolish.

A few words of advice, since that seems to be the privilege of the older generation: startle those around you with smiles and kind words; smile again at the few who will not respond, then go on with those who do. Read a good book, one that uplifts your spirit. Don't fret that someone else has something that you don't—count those things you are blessed with and smile again. Be a friend to all. Keep that friendship within the bounds of social decency—reserve the most intimate acts and conversations for only that one special person that is willing to commit to living up to the standards you establish. Live a life that will bring you to build a marriage and family of honor. Enjoy the fruits of a repentant, forgiving spirit, for we all make mistakes. Allow those around you the benefit of the doubt, for they won't be perfect all the time, either. Turn off the TV, the music, other distractions, and unplug your ears and listen, in this newfound quiet, to your inner self regularly; giving yourself a chance to get to know your spirit. What is it really asking you to do or become? Learn from good leaders how to get there. Start where you are, and move forward with your greatest effort and love for yourself. Above all, be always grateful for all you are, all you can do, all you can become, and express that gratitude often to those who make your life more pleasant.

Now, about that strange title, "Gyrations of Gratitude." On cool mornings when I announce to Chip that it's time to go feed the horses or any other excuse for a romp in the pasture, he runs, bounces, jumps, spins in "gyrations of gratitude" for being able to get out and enjoy. May we be grateful enough to learn from him.

Chapter 81
Grandma Smith

As a summary to this collection of lessons from a variety of sources, I would include a very special lesson from a special person. The earliest real lesson I remember, and the one most indelibly imprinted on my mind, is from Grandmother Smith, the diminutive human that lived in the back bedroom of our house when I was small. She passed away when I was just four, and I only remember one real encounter with her. I had been given a set of toy pistols by my Aunt Marie, and one day as Grandma came out of her room into the living room of our home I pointed one at her and said, "Bang, bang." She came alive, her eyes turned to fire, and she scolded me fiercely. "You will never, young man, point a gun at someone or something unless you mean to kill it!" There was no question as to the meaning or meaningfulness of her words, as I dropped the toy gun and retreated quickly across the room.

I was so ashamed to have offended her. Nobody deserved more respect than this very special person, and I had crossed the line. The effect of that lesson has remained with me all my life. When I was probably ten or so I was playing cowboys and Indians with Stephen Meek on the hill above the house, shooting our cap guns and being as realistic as possible, when I realized that I was pointing the gun not at Stephen, but slightly to the side of him, as I pretended to shoot. I reflected at the time on the lesson from Grandma Smith, and in her honor I consciously continued to point to the side and fire my cap gun, "Bang, bang." I don't think it made any difference to Stephen, as he never knew I was not really aiming at him as the game went on.

The exception to the rule, and one that I actually had to consciously force myself to perform, was when we were shooting with water guns. Because the water was totally harmless I felt it was a safe exception to Grandma's mandate. I got so I was pretty good at water play.

The lesson continues to affect my life as an adult. I have never, nor will I ever, feel good about participating in the "sport" of paintball, where the winner is the one that hits and marks other humans with capsules containing water soluble dye and a gelatin shell propelled from a device called a paintball gun. Harmless, yes, when properly played with protective gear, but in violation of Grandma's rule, so not one that I would enjoy.

Why would a lesson last so long? One that means so much to me not only cannot be forgotten, but will remain uppermost in my mind, for it is impelled by the respect I have for the giver of the lesson—stronger and more lasting than the things I have learned from my bird dogs or the other teachers that affected me throughout my life. I bless her memory for that.

There are lessons to be learned from all people, animals, and things around us, and everything we do, if we are open to learning. This, in fact, is the point: that we all need to be continually learning the lessons in life that will make our lives better, of course in relation to our own satisfaction, but more importantly so that we are more beneficial to those around us. After seventy plus years of learning, I have discovered the important thing is that which we have been taught from our earliest days: there are things of value to our personal growth, development, happiness, and well-being in all that we experience, if we take the time and effort to discover them.

ACKNOWLEDGEMENTS

A very special thanks to Jared Evans, whose enthusiasm for my first bird dog stories gave me the inspiration to collect and compile the rest of them. Thanks to my wife Judy, and to our family, for their unwavering support and cheerleading. Thanks to Jana Botkin for masterful proofing.

Thanks to all those animals, family, and others, whose interactions created lessons from which I learned about life.

ABOUT THE AUTHOR

Dalan Smith was raised on a small Southern Idaho farm, where he learned how to work and play while making his own entertainment. He began working summers for neighboring farmers and ranchers at age twelve, yet realized the value of education to improve one's potential and remained near the top of his class scholastically. Early university studies were on a scientific track, then were switched to business when the development of people became more important to him than researching scientific principles.

Dalan was never prone to follow the path of the multitude. His individualistic ways led to over five decades of primarily self-employment, while supplementing income as necessary with "jobs" from the corporate world, but only long enough to keep financial needs at bay and enable the development of what he really wanted to do, which proved to be motivating people to lift their lives above the usual and inspiring them to reach their full potential.

Dalan developed a successful real estate brokerage with multiple offices and an attached home-building business, while emphasizing to his agents and employees the development of their talents by choosing options with the most benefits to the customer or client, rather than the most money to the agent in the short term.

Writing as a major part of life rather than a hobby began in 2007 after a heart surgery motivated a sale of his businesses and a refocus of efforts to expand the minds and lives of those around him.

Dalan and his wife, Judy, have lived happily in several locations including Bear Lake County, Idaho; Franklin County, Idaho; Morrison, Colorado; Wilson, Wyoming; and Three Rivers, California, most of which enter into the events of this collection, and at this writing are in Emmett, Idaho.

The majority of his continuing efforts to encourage the building of self-confidence and natural ability in those he comes in contact with are directed primarily through his church and supplemented with occasional mailings to those he "adopts".

Made in the USA
Charleston, SC
02 March 2015